E HORNETS 3/12/1993 **52** CLEVELAND CAVALIERS 3/28/199
TONS 3/4/1987 **61** GOLDEN STATE WARRIORS 11/24/1992 49
PPERS 11/21/1997 **49** LOS ANGELES LAKERS 11/20/1992 **54** MIAMI HEAT
VES 11/8/1989 **45** NEW JERSEY NETS 2/26/1987 **58** NEW YORK KNICKS
987 **56** PHOENIX SUNS 1/21/1989 **53** PORTLAND TRAIL BLAZERS 1/8/1987
45 SEATTLE SUPERSONICS 2/2/1997 **45** TORONTO RAPTORS 1/18/1996 **38**
ON WIZARDS 12/23/1992 **57**

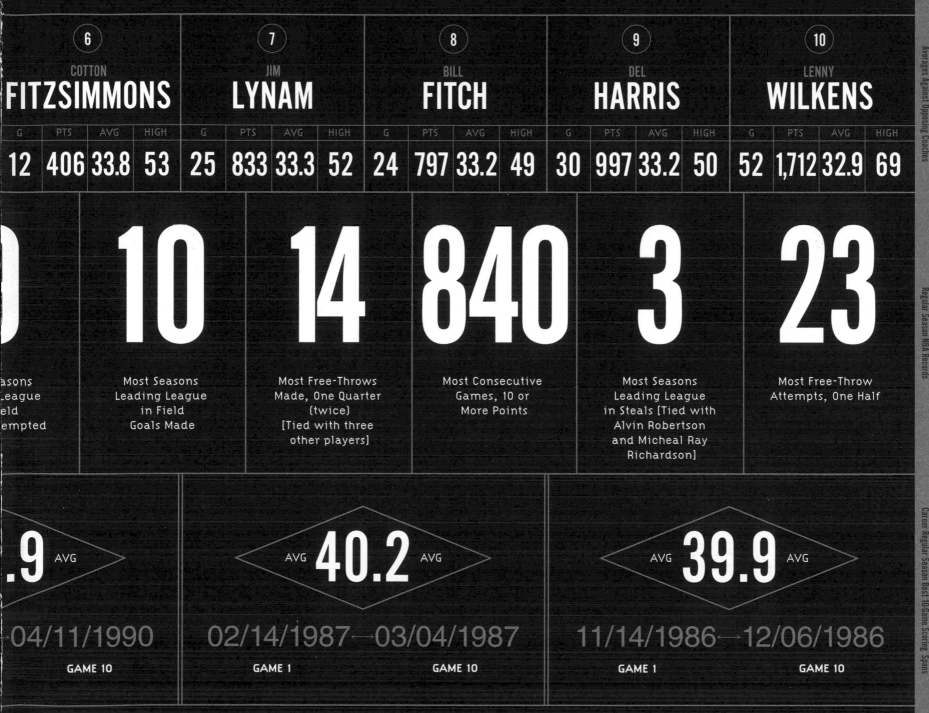

⑥				**⑦**				**⑧**				**⑨**				**⑩**			
COTTON				JIM				BILL				DEL				LENNY			
FITZSIMMONS				**LYNAM**				**FITCH**				**HARRIS**				**WILKENS**			
G	PTS	AVG	HIGH	G	PTS	AVG	HIGH	G	PTS	AVG	HIGH	G	PTS	AVG	HIGH	G	PTS	AVG	HIGH
12	406	33.8	53	25	833	33.3	52	24	797	33.2	49	30	997	33.2	50	52	1,712	32.9	69

	10	**14**	**840**	**3**	**23**
asons eague eld empted	Most Seasons Leading League in Field Goals Made	Most Free-Throws Made, One Quarter (twice) [Tied with three other players]	Most Consecutive Games, 10 or More Points	Most Seasons Leading League in Steals [Tied with Alvin Robertson and Micheal Ray Richardson]	Most Free-Throw Attempts, One Half

.9 AVG

AVG **40.2** AVG

AVG **39.9** AVG

04/11/1990   02/14/1987→03/04/1987   11/14/1986→12/06/1986

GAME 10   GAME 1   GAME 10   GAME 1   GAME 10

/1985 ∂ CHICAGO 121, DETROIT 118 **1986-87 61** 3/4/1987 CHICAGO 125,
8-89 **53** 1/21/1989 PHOENIX 116, ∂ CHICAGO 107 **1989-90 69** 3/28/1990
, MILWAUKEE 94 **1991-92 51** 3/19/1992 CHICAGO 106, ∂ WASHINGTON
55 3/28/1995 CHICAGO 113, ∂ NEW YORK 111 **1995-96 53** 3/7/1996 ∂
K 87 **1997-98 49** 11/21/97 CHICAGO 111, ∂ LOS ANGELES CLIPPERS 102

In memory of my father, James.
your spirit will always run through me.

MJ

FOR THE LOVE OF THE GAME

MY STORY BY MICHAEL JORDAN

Edited by Mark Vancil

CROWN
PUBLISHERS, INC.
NEW YORK

The basketball court was always my refuge. That's where I went when I needed to go somewhere to find an answer to a problem, or just to calm my mind. When I first signed with the Chicago Bulls in 1984, the NBA's Uniform Player's Contract included a clause that prohibited players from certain activities during the offseason, including playing the game. If you played without obtaining permission from the team and were injured, the team could get out of their contract with you. There was no way I could live with that kind of restriction. I needed to play. Not only had I always found comfort on the court, but I used the summer to improve. The Bulls finally agreed to include what I called the

"Love of the Game Clause."

At the time, very few players, if any, had the kind of freedom the Bulls gave me. I could do what I had always done.

I could play the game of basketball without consequence.

I KNEW THE MAGNITUDE OF THE GAME, BUT I DIDN'T FULLY COMPREHEND WHAT IT MEANT. IT WAS 1982 AND I WAS
CHAMPIONSHIP IN THE LOUISIANA SUPERDOME. I REMEMBER RIDING TO THE ARENA. THERE I WAS ABOUT TO FALL
SO RELAXED. I WASN'T COMPLETELY AWAKE AND I WASN'T COMPLETELY ASLEEP. I WAS IN A COMFORTABLE PLACE
SHOT. I COULD SEE MY TEAMMATES: JAMES WORTHY, SAM PERKINS. COACH [DEAN] SMITH. THE DREAM WASN'T
ANOTHER TEAM IN ANOTHER YEAR. BUT AFTER WE BEAT GEORGETOWN FOR THE CHAMPIONSHIP, I TOLD MY FATHER,
YOUR LIFE IS GOING TO CHANGE, SON." I THOUGHT, "WELL, THAT'S JUST MY FATHER TALKING. OF COURSE HE'S GOING

A FRESHMAN AT NORTH CAROLINA. WE WERE PLAYING GEORGETOWN AND PATRICK EWING FOR THE NATIONAL ASLEEP ON THE BUS AND I'M DAYDREAMING ABOUT HITTING A WINNING SHOT. I REMEMBER FEELING SO CALM, SOMEWHERE IN BETWEEN I ENVISIONED BEING THE HERO IN A GAME. I SAW MYSELF HITTING THE GAME-WINNING GAME-SPECIFIC SO I DIDN'T KNOW WHETHER IT WOULD BE AGAINST GEORGETOWN IN A FEW HOURS OR AGAINST ABOUT THE DREAM. HE PAUSED FOR A MOMENT AND SAID "YOUR LIFE WILL NEVER BE THE SAME AFTER THAT SHOT. TO THINK THAT ABOUT HIS SON. AND BESIDES, NO ONE REALLY KNOWS ONE WAY OR ANOTHER."

I NEVER PAID MUCH ATTENTION TO WHAT MY FATHER SAID THAT DAY—UNTIL NOW.

WHEN I THINK OF MY CAREER, WHERE I HAVE COME FROM, WHERE IT ALL BEGAN, AND ALL THAT I HAVE ACCOMPLISHED ALONG THE WAY, I REALIZE EVERYTHING DID CHANGE AFTER THAT GAME. NOT JUST BASKETBALL BUT MY LIFE.

I THINK MY FATHER SAW SOME THINGS IN ME THAT I COULDN'T SEE IN MYSELF.

AT FIRST, I JUST THOUGHT IT WAS A FATHER'S PRIDE, THE VOICING OF HOPES AND DREAMS FOR A SON TO BE SUCCESSFUL. I SAW HIS COMMENTS MORE IN THE CONTEXT OF A MOTIVATIONAL SPEECH A FATHER MIGHT GIVE A SON.

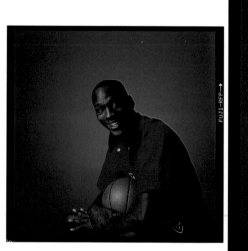  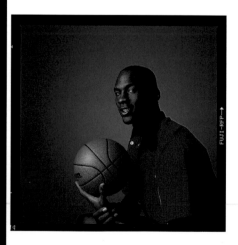

I can't say for sure that way back then he envisioned what would happen to me. But I look at my children now and I can detect certain attributes—which of them is going to be the better athlete, who is going to be more successful, what kind of work they will do. I can tell you some of those things about my children, so I'm pretty sure my father was able to do the same with us. Maybe he could tell whether one of his children had a special talent, a special sense of himself. Maybe he knew one of his sons, for whatever reason, was touched by some special spiritual inspiration.

IN THAT SENSE, I GUESS I WAS THE CHOSEN ONE.

No one from my family is over 6 feet tall. Here I am, 6-foot-6. Where did that come from?

The one chosen to be over 6 feet, something totally out of character for my father and mother?

FUJI—RFP→

You could go back two or three generations and find one person maybe 6-foot-2. But it's not enough that I'm bigger than the norm for my family. I have this special ability. I have an older brother, Larry, who has the same heart, the same kind of ability as I do, and yet he's only 5-foot-8. This is a guy who will still play me one-on-one in a heartbeat. Despite all I've achieved in basketball, Larry believes he can win. Yet he never got the same opportunities. So I think about that now. Why me? I do believe my father knew. I believe he saw things unfolding in a way that no one, not me, not the Chicago Bulls, or anyone else saw. I believe that's a father's gift. I only wish I could talk to him now. How much of all this did he really see?

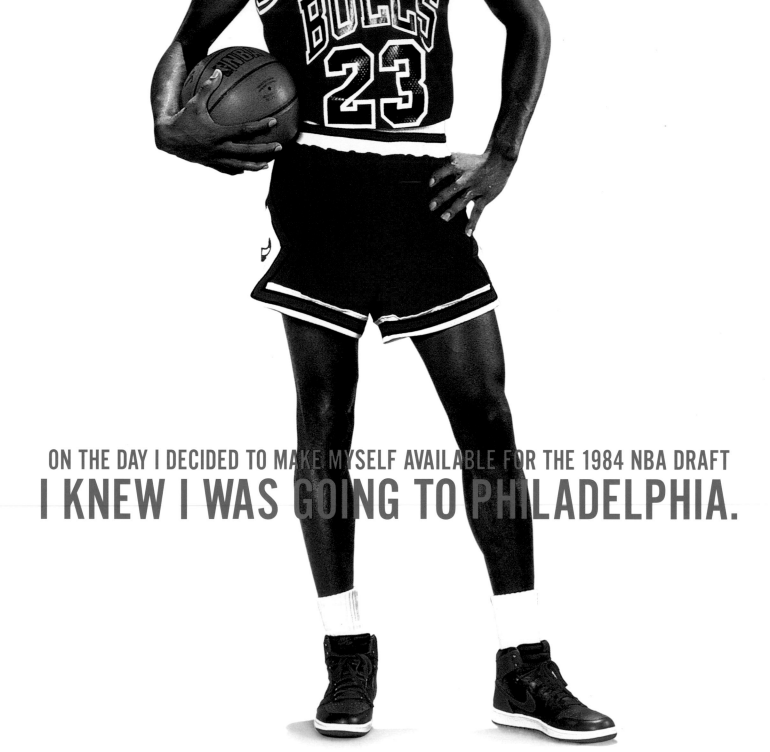

ON THE DAY I DECIDED TO MAKE MYSELF AVAILABLE FOR THE 1984 NBA DRAFT
I KNEW I WAS GOING TO PHILADELPHIA.

I had just finished my junior season at North Carolina and Coach Smith called around the NBA to see how high I'd be drafted if I came out.
At the time, in late March and early April, the 76ers told him they would take me with the second or third pick, depending upon which one they had.
But as the weeks passed, Chicago started losing games and moving up in the draft. Still, the whole thing came down to a coin flip for the No. 1 pick.
The NBA didn't have the draft lottery at the time, so a coin flip between the worst team from each conference decided the first pick. The rest of the league
lined up behind the first two teams with the third pick going to the team with the third worst record and so on. If Portland had won the flip, it was going to take
Hakeem Olajuwon. I would have gone to Houston and Sam Bowie would have ended up in Chicago, which lost enough to pass Philadelphia. When Houston won
the flip the Rockets took Hakeem and Portland went for Bowie. The funny thing is the Bulls had lost a coin flip in 1979 with the Los Angeles Lakers.
The Lakers took Magic Johnson and the Bulls selected David Greenwood, who was still with the team when I arrived.

AMAZING, ISN'T IT? A SIMPLE FLIP OF A COIN.

1984 Top 5 Draft Picks

Pos.	Player	Team	All-Star	Championships
1.	Hakeem Olajuwon	Houston	13	2
2.	Sam Bowie	Portland	0	0
3.	Michael Jordan	Chicago	12	6
4.	Sam Perkins	Dallas	0	0
5.	Charles Barkley	Philadelphia	12	0

I do believe there are things going on in the world that none of us can see. I know it's true in my life. The only school I was interested in out of high school was UCLA. All they had to do was call and I would have been there. But they never recruited me, so I went to North Carolina. It turned out to be the perfect decision because I was able to play for Coach Smith, who taught me the importance of fundamentals. Then, when I decided to turn pro in 1984, the Olympic Games were not only in the United States, but in Los Angeles, which guaranteed everyone high visibility. I could have ended up in Portland or Houston, but I landed in the middle of the country in one of the three major markets. Kevin Loughery was probably the perfect first coach and Chicago was probably the perfect situation. Loughery had coached Julius Erving in the American Basketball Association, so he understood my skills and provided me with the freedom to develop. At the same time, Dr. J was leaving and Larry Bird and Magic Johnson were there to take the focus off me. It wasn't like I was Grant Hill or Shaquille O'Neal coming into the NBA with expectations of carrying an entire league. If I had gone to Portland I don't think I would have developed as fast because Clyde Drexler and Jim Paxson were there. Away from the game, my impact would have been entirely different. Chicago made a big difference for everything that occurred off the court. The city of Chicago embraces great players. Nike would not have been able to promote me to the extent it was able to in Chicago. I will always believe that wherever I had gone my skills eventually would have been acknowledged. But off the court, it wouldn't have been the same. So when you look at all those twists and turns, all the little things that happened and turned out to be major events, I have to believe there was an original rhythm to my life, a spiritual road that I was traveling without ever knowing where it would lead.

WHEN I CAME INTO THE LEAGUE, I WASN'T NEARLY AS ENAMORED
WITH MAGIC JOHNSON AND LARRY BIRD AS I WAS WITH JULIUS ERVING.

AS A KID MY FIRST NICKNAME WAS MAGIC, BUT
THE ONLY PLAYER I REALLY KNEW ABOUT WAS DR. J.

I HAD A COUPLE GOOD GAMES AGAINST PHILADELPHIA MY FIRST SEASON, BUT I COULDN'T DO ANYTHING
WHEN I WAS MATCHED AGAINST JULIUS BECAUSE I HAD SO MUCH ADMIRATION FOR HIM.
I WAS JUST HAPPY TO BE ON THE SAME FLOOR.

Michael Jeffrey Jordan	MJ	DrJ	Julius Winfield Erving II
February 17, 1963	Birth Date		February 22, 1950
Brooklyn, New York	Birthplace		Roosevelt, New York
Chicago Bulls	First Team		Virginia Squires
NBA	League		ABA
21	Rookie Age		21
28.2	Scoring		27.3
6.5	Rebounds		15.7
5.9	Assists		4.0
51.5%	Shooting		50.1%
84.5%	FT Shooting		74.5%

Ⓐ T THE TIME, HE WAS THE KING WHEN IT CAME TO A PROFESSIONAL BASKETBALL PLAYER MOVING INTO CORPORATE AMERICA. HIS COCA-COLA CONNECTION WAS LIKE THE CONNECTION I EVENTUALLY HAD WITH NIKE. IN THAT SENSE, DR. J MADE IT POSSIBLE FOR ME TO TAKE THE NEXT STEP OFF THE COURT. HE BROUGHT SO MUCH CLASS TO THE PROFESSIONAL ATHLETE. IN THE 1950S AND 1960S, YOU HAD PEOPLE LIKE JOE DIMAGGIO AND JACKIE ROBINSON. BUT JULIUS ERVING WAS THE FIRST BASKET-BALL PLAYER TO COMBINE DRAMATIC ATHLETIC ABILITY ON THE COURT WITH A CLEAN, POSITIVE IMAGE OFF THE COURT THAT CONNECTED WITH CORPORATE AMERICA.

I NEVER WANTED TO SIGN WITH NIKE.

I had been an Adidas fanatic since high school. In fact, I didn't even want to meet with Nike. In the summer of 1984, I had been flying all over the country for various awards banquets, the Bulls, and the Olympics. I was tired of traveling. When it came time to meet with Nike, I told everyone, my agent David Falk, Coach Smith, even my parents, that I wasn't going. I had no intention of signing with Nike and I had no desire to fly to Portland, Oregon.

My parents finally sat me down and said, "This is important. You need to listen to what those people have to say." I felt like I was dragged out to Oregon to listen to something I had no intention of acting upon. So I walk into the meeting and there's Rob Strasser, Phil Knight, Tinker Hatfield, Jack George, Peter Moore, and Howard White. Now I'm not pleased about being there and I'm barely listening. But Strasser got my attention. They were talking about giving me my own shoe and effectively redefining the entire athletic shoe industry. Strasser did most of the talking. He was a big guy, smooth, energetic, and motivating. Still, I was skeptical because **I didn't even like Nike shoes.** The money was substantial for that time, $250,000 a year for five years with an annuity, incentives, and royalties on all Nike basketball-related items. It was a great deal, but it also was risky because no one in the industry had done anything like that. Julius Erving became identified with a specific shoe, but he was never compensated the way I was going to be. Growing up, everyone would say, "I want a pair of Dr. J's." They were Converse shoes. In retrospect, **they squeezed the equity out of Julius Erving without ever**

From the beginning, David Falk understood the potential at Nike and how that deal could be used as a model for other marketing partners. Nike did too. What Nike didn't know at the time was how much I was going to be involved in the evolution of the product and how much I loved the creative process. Also, no one knew how well I would play. I didn't even know. I had no idea.

paying for it. The meeting was interesting, but when it ended I'm thinking, "Fine, now let's go see what Converse has in mind. Then I'm going to sign with Adidas."

Before I went to Converse I talked to Bill Sweek, a sales rep from Adidas I had met at North Carolina. I did this on my own. **No one, including Falk, knew about my meeting with Bill.** I told him what Nike was offering and said, "All you have to do is come close." In the meantime I had to see Converse, which was a very traditional, conservative company. Converse had Magic Johnson, Isiah Thomas, Larry Bird, Mark Aguirre, Dr. J, all the top players. I met with them at their corporate headquarters outside Boston. The place just looked traditional and I really didn't feel comfortable there. But I had some experience with Converse because we wore them for games at North Carolina and I felt obligated to listen. Their offer was pennies compared to the dimes Nike was offering. Their top guys were all making $100,000 a year and Dr. J wasn't even making royalties on his shoe. They were afraid of making an exception with me, which I understood. Besides, I **wasn't comfortable with Converse. I remember having bad vibes.**

My heart was still with Adidas, but they never made an offer. They didn't want to take a chance on the U.S. basketball market because they didn't want to jeopardize the international brand. The decision was a lot easier for Nike. The company's stock had dropped by more than half and was down around $6 a share in 1984. Strasser had to take a gamble. And he did. He wanted to change the entire market by betting on one person. **Nike didn't have a second choice.** He was a genius. It worked.

GROSS REVENUES IN 1984
$986,000,000

GROSS REVENUES IN 1998
$9,186,539,000

WAS IT THE SHOES?

COST OF ONE SHARE OF NIKE
STOCK ON NOVEMBER 1, 1984

$7.00

VALUE OF THAT SHARE
AS OF JULY 2, 1998

$418.00

$5,000.00

FINE PER GAME

NIKE HAD AN ADVERTISING CAMPAIGN IN MIND, BUT THEY WERE AFRAID TO PUT IT INTO MOTION UNTIL THEY SAW ME PLAY. I STARTED THE 1984–85 SEASON WEARING THE BLACK AND RED SHOE. THREE GAMES INTO THE SEASON, THE NBA DID US A HUGE FAVOR. THE LEAGUE BANNED THE SHOE BECAUSE IT DIDN'T CONFORM TO THE REST OF THE BULLS UNIFORM. BUT I KEPT WEARING THEM AND DAVID STERN STARTED FINING ME. I THINK IT STARTED OUT AT $1,000 A GAME, THEN WENT TO $3,000, AND EVENTUALLY $5,000. NIKE DIDN'T BLINK. NIKE SAID THEY WERE WILLING TO PAY EVERY PENNY AND I TOTALLY AGREED. IT WOULD HAVE COST MILLIONS OF DOLLARS TO COME UP WITH A PROMOTION THAT PRODUCED AS MUCH PUBLICITY AS THE LEAGUE'S BAN DID. THE WHOLE THING WORKED PERFECTLY. THE FIRST COMMERCIAL SHOWED MY HEAD, AND THE CAMERA SLOWLY MOVED DOWN MY BODY TO MY FEET. WHEN THE CAMERA HIT THE SHOES A BIG "X" WAS STAMPED ON THE SCREEN AND THE ANNOUNCER SAID, "BANNED." RIGHT AFTER THAT, SALES WENT CRAZY.

MY ATTITUDE GOING INTO TRAINING CAMP AS A ROOKIE WAS TO IMPRESS.

I wanted to impress my teammates, my coaches, the owners, everybody. I wanted them to say, "This kid is special. This kid has the right mind, the right skills, the right motivation." All my effort that first year was geared toward proving myself. I went as hard as I could all the time. I tried to win every drill, every scrimmage. I tried to dominate, but never vocally. I felt until I earned the right to speak I wasn't going to say a word. I was the second-highest-paid player on the team, but I never wore that on my sleeve. I didn't go out and buy cars and clothes like rookies today. I always tried to dress nice, but I never wanted to be the best-dressed. Not even close. I lived very modestly. Away from the game I wanted to fit in. But on the court

I WAS NEVER BOTHERED BY EXPECTATIONS OTHERS HAD FOR ME BECAUSE I WAS FOCUSED ON MYSELF. I DIDN'T KNOW WHAT IT TOOK TO PROVE YOU BELONGED. WAS IT STATISTICS? WAS IT THE CONFIDENCE YOU SHOWED? WAS IT FITTING IN WITH THE NBA LIFESTYLE? EVERYTHING WAS COMPLETELY UNKNOWN.

Players who led their teams (outright) in points per game, assists per game, total rebounds per game, and steals per game in the same season.

Season	Player	Team	Pts	Ast	Rb	Stl
1996–97	Grant Hill	Detroit	21.4	7.3	9.0	1.8
1995–96	Grant Hill	Detroit	20.2	6.9	9.8	1.3
1994–95	Scottie Pippen	Chicago	21.4	5.2	8.1	2.9
1989–90	Lafayette Lever	Denver	18.3	6.5	9.3	2.1
1985–86	Larry Bird	Boston	25.8	6.8	9.8	2.0
● 1984–85	Michael Jordan	Chicago	28.2	5.9	6.5	2.4
1977–78	Dave Cowens	Boston	18.6	4.6	14.0	1.3
1975–76	George McGinnis	Phil.	23.0	4.7	12.6	2.6

● ROOKIE

THE 1984–85 BULLS TEAM HAD AS MUCH
RAW TALENT AS ANY OF OUR CHAMPIONSHIP TEAMS.

BUT IT WAS ALL POTENTIAL.

Most of them didn't have any idea how to win. Some were looking for that kind of leadership from me, others were not. Guys like Sidney Green, Orlando Woolridge, and David Greenwood were naturally talented, but they weren't basketball players. Dave Corzine was a basketball player. He couldn't run or jump, but he knew how to play the game. Rod Higgins was a solid all-around player and he understood the game. Greenwood? He was in it for the money. He never wanted to

couldn't miss a practice much less a game. From my first day in the league to my last, I always felt I had a lot to prove. The only difference between 1984 and 1998 was the expectations of everyone around the game. But my expectations never changed. The better I got the better I wanted to become. But there were a lot of things going on with that first team. Everyone knows there were players doing drugs. I still mingled with my teammates, but I wasn't going where they were

push himself beyond his comfort zone. I remember twisting my ankle in practice the day before a game. It swelled up pretty good, but I never thought it was bad enough to prevent me from playing. Greenwood walked by as I was getting treatment and said, "With that ankle it would be a week before I played." The idea of not playing never crossed my mind. I was thinking about how I would compensate, how I would get around the fact I wouldn't be 100 percent. I noticed right off that my appetite for success was much bigger than that of a lot of players. I was motivated because I wanted to succeed. I

going. And I wasn't tempted by what was going on around me. I was surprised by some of the people doing drugs, but the act didn't shock me. I remember thinking, "So this is what professional basketball is about. Doing drugs and trying to play the game." I could see how players could get misguided if they were weak-minded. I wasn't a snitch and I never allowed the extracurricular stuff to break my bond with the team. I decided I was going to go out there and let the fans decide the winners and losers. My father always told me, "The cream always rises if you put forth the effort." That was my focus.

I WAS VERY AWARE OF WHAT I HAD DONE ON THE COURT ~~IN THE FORST~~ HALF OF MY ROOKIE YEAR. THE LAST THING I WANTED TO DO AT THE

1985 ALL-STAR GAME

WAS DRAW EVEN MORE ATTENTION TO MYSELF.

I BROUGHT MY FAMILY WITH ME TO INDIANAPOLIS AND ALL I PLANNED TO DO WAS SOAK IN THE ATMOSPHERE, MEET THE PLAYERS, AND PLAY THE GAME. MY MINDSET WAS TO BLEND IN AND NOT MAKE WAVES. EXACTLY WHAT I WAS TRYING TO AVOID HAPPENED ANYWAY. I BROKE OUT THE FIRST NIKE AIR JORDAN SWEATS DURING THE SLAM-DUNK COMPETITION AND CERTAIN PLAYERS, ISIAH THOMAS AND DOMINIQUE WILKINS FOR STARTERS, THOUGHT I WAS BEING DISRESPECTFUL. I THOUGHT I WAS DOING NIKE A FAVOR. THEY HAD INVESTED SO MUCH IN ME AND I FIGURED WEARING THE WARM-UPS WOULD BE GOOD FOR THE COMPANY.

1984-85
All NBA First/Second Teams

FIRST Team

Larry Bird, Boston

Bernard King, New York

Moses Malone, Philadelphia

Magic Johnson, L.A. Lakers

Isiah Thomas, Detroit

SECOND Team

Terry Cummings, Milwaukee

Ralph Sampson, Houston

Kareem Abdul-Jabbar, L.A. Lakers

Michael Jordan, Chicago

Sidney Moncrief, Milwaukee

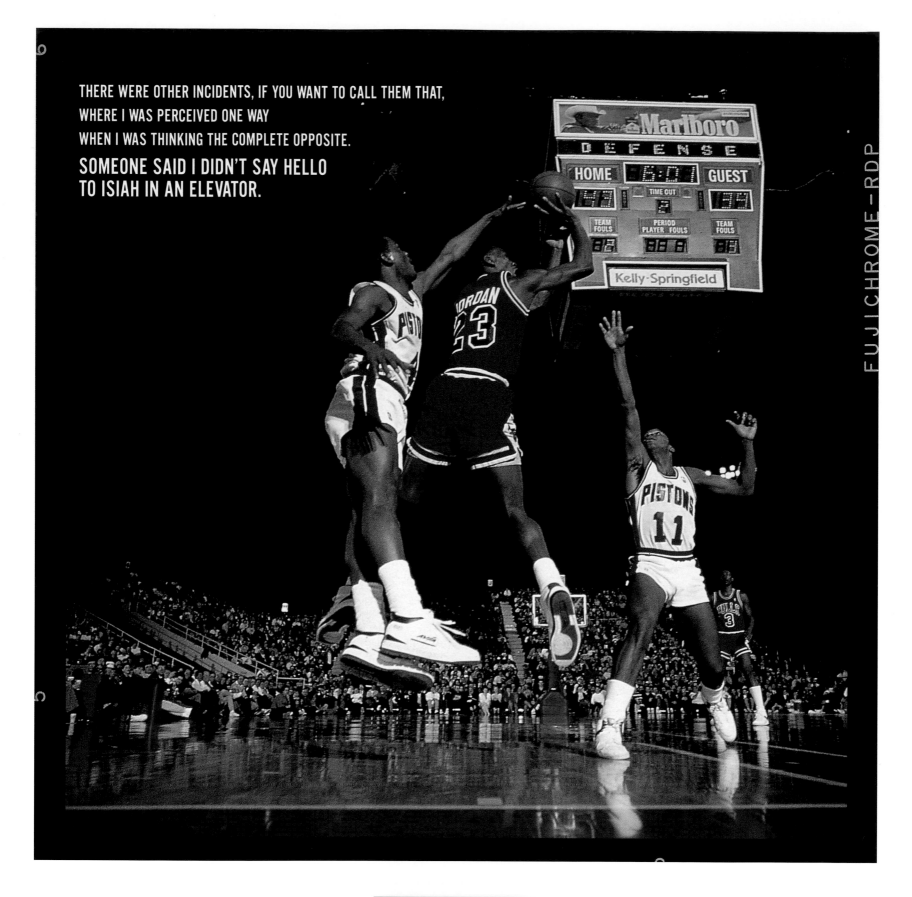

THERE WERE OTHER INCIDENTS, IF YOU WANT TO CALL THEM THAT,
WHERE I WAS PERCEIVED ONE WAY
WHEN I WAS THINKING THE COMPLETE OPPOSITE.
SOMEONE SAID I DIDN'T SAY HELLO
TO ISIAH IN AN ELEVATOR.

FUJICHROME-RDP

But there was a reason. I was in an elevator full of great players and I was afraid to say anything. I didn't want to come off as being too confident, so I didn't say a word. The next day I'm back in Chicago and a reporter comes up to me after practice and tells me about the freeze-out. He said Isiah, George Gervin, and some other players were laughing about how they had tried to embarrass me during the game by freezing me out, or not giving me the ball. I didn't notice a thing, to tell you the truth. But that incident was one of the most painful experiences of my life to that point. I was so disillusioned I didn't know what to do. I called my parents and talked to them for a long time. I knew that everything

FUJICHROME-RDP

happened for a purpose and I could either learn from the experience or fight it. I decided to do both. The next night we played Detroit at home and I played like I was possessed. We beat the Pistons in overtime in a very physical game. There were a couple near fights and I had my first real run-in with Bill Laimbeer. But there was no way I was going to let us lose

that game. I scored 49 points and had 15 rebounds. I also got a piece of Isiah's last-second shot that could have tied the game. I guess you could say our rivalry with Detroit suddenly had a foundation. For the next seven years I would do all I could to build upon that foundation. I'm pretty sure Isiah and Laimbeer had the same idea.

WHAT WENT ON BETWEEN
JERRY KRAUSE,
JERRY REINSDORF,
AND ME DURING THE 1985–86 SEASON
WAS SOMETHING I NEVER GOT OVER.
I NOW LOOK AT THAT SITUATION
AS A TEST,
MAYBE THE BIGGEST TEST
OF MY PROFESSIONAL CAREER.
BUT IT ALSO GAVE ME A VERY CLEAR VIEW
OF KRAUSE AND REINSDORF.

REGULAR SEASON GAMES MISSED DUE
TO INJURY, SICKNESS, OR SUSPENSION
1985–86

64 of 82

REGULAR SEASON GAMES MISSED DUE
TO INJURY, SICKNESS, OR SUSPENSION
1984–85/1986–98

7 of 848

THEY WERE BUSINESSMEN.
THEY WERE NOT SPORTSMEN
AND THEY DIDN'T HAVE A TRUE APPRECIATION
FOR THE GAME.

THEY MADE BUSINESS DECISIONS
AND BASKETBALL JUST HAPPENED
TO BE THE BUSINESS.

I broke the navicular bone in my left foot during a game at Golden State in the third game of my second season. The initial X-rays didn't show a thing. I kept taking treatment and trying to play, but I could hardly walk. A CAT scan, which showed the bone in layers, eventually detected the break. I couldn't believe it. I went home and cried for days. I was so depressed my father flew in from North Carolina because my parents were worried about me. After seven weeks, I was told the crack hadn't healed enough. I was demoralized all over again because I thought for sure I'd be back by the All-Star break. But I convinced the doctor to give me a removable splint instead of another cast. That's all I needed. I went back to North Carolina where I was taking a class and I started speeding up the rehabilitation process. The Bulls had me see two orthopedic specialists in addition to John Hefferon, the team's orthopedic surgeon. On February 12 I was back in Chicago for an evaluation. But Reinsdorf and Krause still didn't want me to play. We had a late-night meeting with all the doctors on a speaker phone. None of them wanted to be the one to say it was safe for me to play. So I went back to North Carolina and started playing anyway. I shot baskets for a few days, played some light one-on-one, then two-on-two, then full-court games. In a four-week period I played myself back into shape and no one knew a thing about it. The next time I came back the doctors couldn't believe the results of the strength test. My left leg was actually stronger than my right. So we had another meeting, same office. Reinsdorf, Krause, and I sat down at the table. Before anybody could say a word, I said, "I don't want there to be any confusion." I reached into my briefcase and pulled out a tape recorder and

set it right in the middle of the table. Once again, the doctors backed off. Dr. Stan James told us there was a 10 percent chance I could break the bone again. That was all Reinsdorf and Krause wanted to hear. The team was lousy and they were thinking about a lottery pick. They were very careful not to say those exact words, but they might as well have written them on the wall. That's when the argument began. Krause said, "We're not taking the chance. What are you thinking?" I said, "My thinking is there's a 90

percent chance I won't break it again." But I knew those guys had a completely different agenda. And I broke it out right there in front of them: "You're trying to lose games so you can get a better draft pick." That hit a nerve with Krause. This was right around the time Tylenol capsules coated with cyanide were found. So Reinsdorf gives me this scenario: "What if I gave you 10 pills in a bottle and one of them was coated with cyanide? Would you reach in and take the risk of grabbing the wrong pill?" I thought for a moment and said, "You know

what, Jerry, that's a hell of an analogy. But my answer is this: it depends on how bad the headache is." Reinsdorf wanted a 100 percent guarantee, but I didn't have a 100 percent chance of remaining healthy when I broke the bone in the first place. Besides, if it broke again I'd have plenty of time for surgery before training camp. If I didn't test the foot now and it broke later on, then I'd lose another season. But I was in this battle all by myself. Even Falk was on their side. Everyone was worried about the Golden Goose while I'm worrying about life at that moment. By the end of the night, Reinsdorf and Krause agreed to let me practice at full speed, but they limited my game time to seven minutes a half. I could practice two hours a day, but I couldn't play more than seven minutes? These were the same guys who called me the greatest practice player they'd ever seen. Reinsdorf and Krause made up this ridiculous system that increased my time by a minute per half each game. It should have been embarrassing for the entire league much less the team. One night we're playing at Indiana and we have the ball with 31 seconds left in the game and we're losing by a point. The night before Reinsdorf had called coach Stan Albeck and told him if I played one minute too long he would be fired. Now my minutes are done. If two seconds click off the clock, then my time rounds up another minute. Stan takes me out of the game. The fans are going crazy. They're yelling at Stan, calling him names. I'm at the end of the bench and I'm furious. John Paxson eventually hit a game-winning shot at the buzzer. But right there I knew all I needed to know about Reinsdorf and Krause.

"I THINK HE'S GOD DISGUISED AS MICHAEL JORDAN.

HE IS THE MOST AWESOME PLAYER IN THE NBA.

TODAY IN BOSTON GARDEN, ON NATIONAL TV, IN THE PLAYOFFS,

HE PUT ON ONE OF THE GREATEST SHOWS OF ALL TIME.

I COULDN'T BELIEVE SOMEONE COULD DO THAT

AGAINST THE BOSTON CELTICS."

LARRY BIRD, APRIL 21, 1986

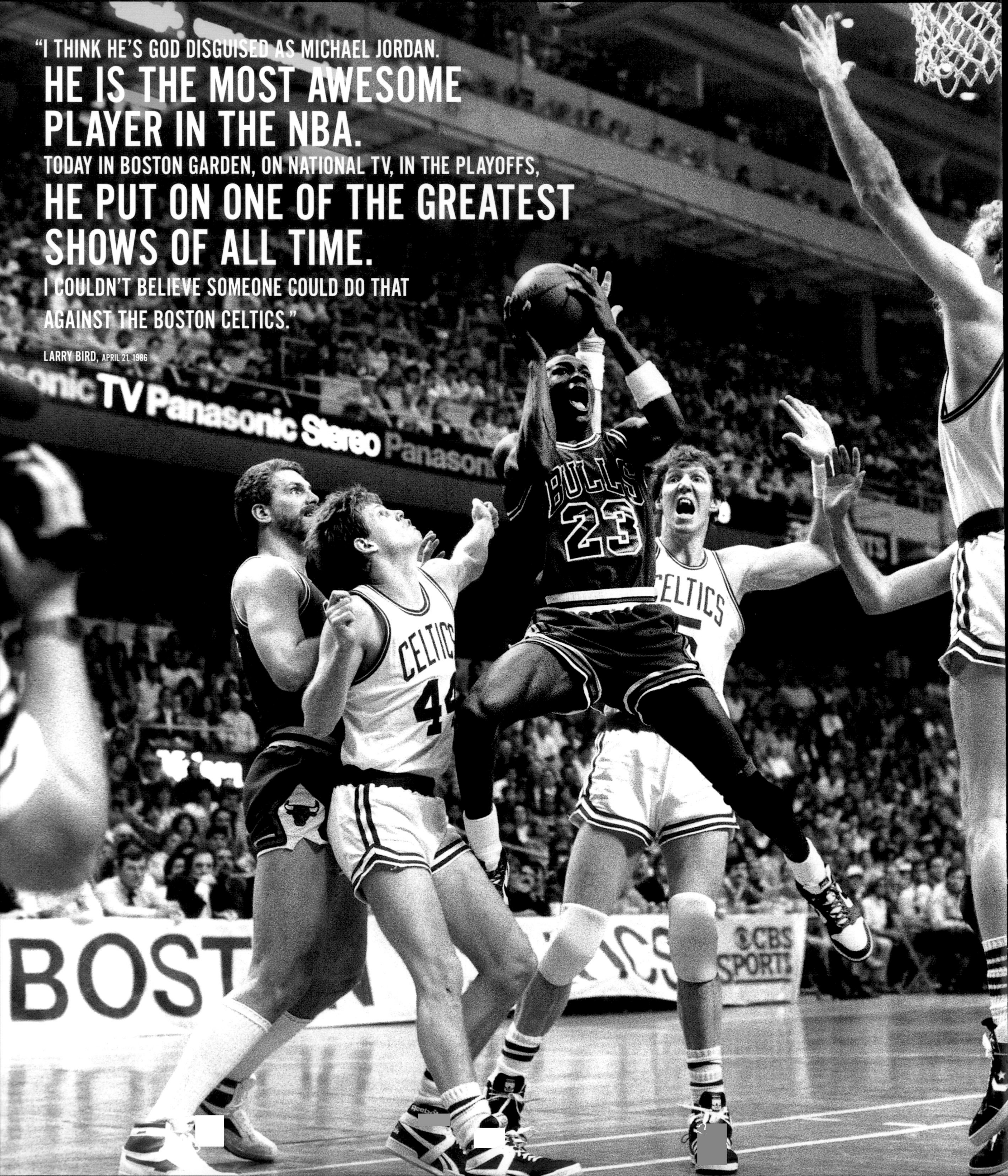

I REMEMBER READING WHAT LARRY SAID ABOUT THAT GAME.
I REALLY COULDN'T BELIEVE HE WOULD SAY SOMETHING LIKE THAT.
HERE WAS A GUY WHO HAD BEEN IN THE LEAGUE SEVEN YEARS AND WAS IN A CLASS I WAS TRYING TO ENTER.
TO THAT POINT I DON'T THINK I HAD EVER PLAYED A GAME AS GOOD AS THAT ONE.
BUT I KNEW I STILL HAD A LONG WAY TO GO.

MICHAEL JORDAN—BOSTON GARDEN 1986 NBA PLAYOFFS GAME 2

53	22	41	19	21	5	6	3	2	63
MINUTES	FG	FGA	FT	FTA	REBOUNDS	ASSISTS	STEALS	BLOCKS	POINTS

arry Bird's comments gave me credibility. Up to that point I was still perceived as a hotshot rookie, not a real player. When Bird acknowledged my performance, I became a player. I still wasn't up to his level, but I was now a player who was marked as a star, a potential Hall of Famer depending upon how I took those comments. At the time, I really didn't understand what his statements meant to me. In other words, his praise wasn't going to change how I would try to establish myself as a player. I didn't see myself in the same way Larry did. If I did, I probably wouldn't have accomplished as much as I did later. I took those words as a compliment and nothing more. He confirmed I was on the right path, but nothing he or anyone else might have said would have altered that path. Off the court, Larry Bird intimidated me because of who he was, what he had accomplished, and the fact that he was Larry Legend. I felt the same way

about all the stars at that time: Magic Johnson, Julius Erving, all of them. I wasn't scared of them on the court because I believed I had the skills to compete with anybody. But their presence off the court intimidated me. Now that I look back I realize how much I had to learn to attain their level. I'm glad I didn't know then how much I had yet to learn. If I hadn't evolved at my own pace, I wouldn't have been able to paint the tiny details that defined my career. I remember every little step, every little crease. Now when I look back I see one big beautiful picture. Some of these young kids just have that big blob of paint without any detail. Their careers are just a mass of color without any definition because they haven't taken the time to work on the details or they don't appreciate or understand the process.

D OUG COLLINS AND I GOT OFF ON THE WRONG FOOT. STAN ALBECK HAD BEEN FIRED AND KRAUSE BROUGHT IN COLLINS, WHO HAD BEEN SECRETLY SCOUTING THE TEAM FOR THE FINAL MONTH OF THE 1985–86 SEASON. I HAD ONE LAST CAT SCAN ON MY LEFT FOOT BEFORE LEAVING FOR THE SUMMER. BEFORE I LEFT, KRAUSE WANTED ME TO MEET DOUG. WE SAT DOWN AND KRAUSE SAID HE DIDN'T WANT ME PLAYING BASKETBALL THAT SUMMER. I LOOKED HIM RIGHT IN THE EYE AND SAID, "LOOK, I'M GOING BACK TO NORTH CAROLINA TO PLAY BASKETBALL. THAT'S HOW I IMPROVE. I HAVE TO PLAY BASKETBALL IN THE SUMMER. BESIDES, I FINISHED THE SEASON PLAYING MORE THAN 40 MINUTES A GAME." KRAUSE SAID, "YOU ARE THE BULLS PROPERTY AND WE CAN TELL YOU WHAT YOU CAN DO AND WHAT YOU CAN'T DO." DOUG COLLINS' WAS RIGHT THERE AND HE REITERATED THE SAME THOUGHT. ACTUALLY, DOUG MIGHT HAVE SAID IT FIRST WITH KRAUSE BACKING HIM UP. EITHER WAY, BOTH OF THEM WERE RIGHT THERE IN MY FACE. IF I PLAYED IN ANY GAMES THEY SAID THEY WOULD FINE ME. I SAID, "YOU DON'T CONTROL MY TIME. THE SUMMER IS MY TIME. EIGHT MONTHS OF THE YEAR I WORK FOR THE CHICAGO BULLS. BUT I AM NOT ANYBODY'S PROPERTY." I STORMED OUT. A FEW WEEKS LATER THEY HEARD I WAS GOING TO PLAY IN A UNLV-NORTH CAROLINA ALUMNI GAME IN LAS VEGAS. I WAS REBELLIOUS, BUT I WASN'T CRAZY. AND I DIDN'T WANT ANY MORE STRAIN WITH MANAGEMENT. I TOLD COACH SMITH AND THE ALUMNI PEOPLE I'D GO OUT TO UNLV TO SUPPORT THE TEAM, BUT I WOULDN'T PLAY. NO SOONER DID I GET TO LAS VEGAS THAN KRAUSE SENDS A MESSAGE TO MY ROOM. "I KNOW YOU'RE NOT GOING TO PLAY, BUT IF YOU DO WE'RE GOING TO FINE YOU THE MAXIMUM WE CAN FINE YOU AS A CHICAGO BULLS PLAYER." NOW I'M STEAMING. I GET TO THE ARENA AND THERE THEY ARE, KRAUSE AND COLLINS SIT- TING IN THE FRONT ROW. THEY CAME ALL THE WAY TO LAS VEGAS TO SEE IF I WAS GOING TO PLAY AFTER THEY KNEW I HAD NO PLANS TO PLAY. THE NORTH CAROLINA TEAM IS IN THE LOCKER ROOM JUST ABOUT READY TO COME OUT. I TOOK ONE LOOK AT KRAUSE AND COLLINS AND MARCHED RIGHT INTO THE LOCKER ROOM AND SAID, "GIVE ME A UNIFORM." THEY STILL TRIED TO FINE ME, BUT THEY COULDN'T BECAUSE OF THE "LOVE OF THE GAME" CLAUSE IN MY CONTRACT. I ALWAYS WONDERED WHY THEY WENT TO ALL THAT TROUBLE? WHAT WAS THE POINT? WHAT WAS THEIR MOTIVATION? WERE THEY TRYING TO BREAK MY SPIRIT? KRAUSE TREATED EVERYBODY LIKE A PIECE OF MEAT AND HE TRIED TO DO THE SAME WITH ME.

WHAT HE DIDN'T KNOW AND
WHAT HE COULD NEVER TOUCH
WAS MY SENSE OF MYSELF.

I HAD SELF-RESPECT AND NOTHING ANYONE COULD DO TO ME
OR SAY ABOUT ME COULD CHANGE THAT.

IT WOULD HAVE BEEN TOUGH, IF NOT IMPOSSIBLE, TO KEEP SCORING LIKE I DID DURING THE 1986–87 SEASON. I ATTACKED FROM THE OPENING TIP UNTIL THE LAST WHISTLE FOR 82 GAMES. THAT WAS MY MENTALITY. IN TERMS OF PHYSICAL TALENT WE PROBABLY HAD LESS ON THAT TEAM THAN ANY OTHER BULLS TEAM I PLAYED ON. OUR STARTING LINE-UP WHEN THE SEASON OPENED WAS STEVE COLTER AT POINT GUARD, EARL CURETON AND CHARLES OAKLEY AT FORWARDS, AND GRANVILLE WAITERS AT CENTER. I KNEW I NEEDED TO SCORE IF WE WERE GOING TO BE SUCCESSFUL. I'M PRETTY SURE DOUG COLLINS FELT THE SAME WAY. I HAD ONE STREAK OF NINE STRAIGHT GAMES WITH 40 OR MORE POINTS. YOU HAVE NO IDEA HOW MUCH ENERGY IT TAKES TO SCORE 40 POINTS ONE NIGHT. THE DIFFERENCE BETWEEN AVERAGING 32 POINTS A GAME OVER AN ENTIRE SEASON VERSUS A LITTLE

40-Point Game Streak

November 28, 1986 @ L.A. Lakers
41

November 29, 1986 @ Golden State
40

December 2, 1986 @ Seattle
40

December 3, 1986 @ Utah
45

December 5, 1986 @ Phoenix
43

December 6, 1986 @ San Antonio
43

December 9, 1986 @ Denver
40

December 10, 1986 @ Atlanta
41

December 12, 1986 @ Milwaukee
41

OVER 37 IS SIGNIFICANT. THINK OF IT THIS WAY: IF I SCORED 32 ONE NIGHT THEN I HAD TO SCORE 42 THE NEXT NIGHT JUST TO GET EVEN. BUT THAT WAS A DIFFERENT ERA. VERY FEW TEAMS WERE AS SOPHISTICATED DEFENSIVELY AS THEY ARE TODAY. AND NO TEAM, WITH THE EXCEPTION OF DETROIT THE NEXT SEASON, GEARED ITS ENTIRE DEFENSIVE GAMEPLAN TO SHUTTING DOWN ONE PLAYER. THAT'S WHY I'VE ALWAYS SAID WILT CHAMBERLAIN NEVER COULD AVERAGE 50 POINTS A GAME TODAY. HE COULDN'T EVEN LEAD THE LEAGUE IN SCORING. WHAT COULD I HAVE SCORED PLAYING AGAINST JOHN STOCKTON EVERY NIGHT WITH NO DOUBLE TEAMS? I'D STAND IN THE POST AND SCORE EVERY TIME I TOUCHED THE BALL. THAT'S NOT MUCH DIFFERENT THAN WHAT WILT DID. YOU WANT TO SEE WILT CHAMBERLAIN IN TODAY'S GAME? LOOK AT SHAQUILLE O'NEAL. THAT'S A MODERN VERSION.

	MOST CONSECUTIVE GAMES, 40 OR MORE POINTS			MOST GAMES, 40 OR MORE POINTS, SEASON		
14	10	9	63	52	37
Wilt Chamberlain, Philadelphia Dec. 8–Dec. 30, 1961 Jan. 11–Feb. 1, 1962	Wilt Chamberlain, San Francisco Nov. 9–Nov. 25, 1962	Michael Jordan, Chicago Nov. 28–Dec. 12, 1986	Wilt Chamberlain, Philadelphia 1961–62	Wilt Chamberlain, San Francisco 1962–63	Michael Jordan, Chicago 1986–87

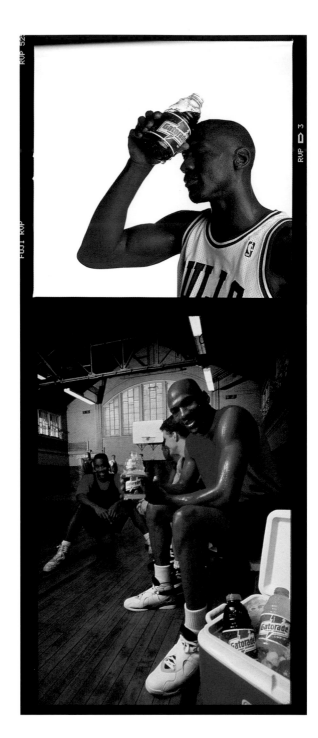

It wasn't until 1988 that I understood the level I was playing at and the magnitude of the business decisions off the court. Before the 1987–88 season I was trying to make my mark. I was focused on proving I belonged in that upper echelon with Magic and Larry. Off the court, my first deals were starting to come up for renegotiation. I was making the transition from Coca-Cola to Gatorade and there were more deals on the table at substantially more dollars. By 1988 I had a very clear understanding of the business of basketball. I had tried to learn as much as possible about every deal. From the initial concept through the negotiations and into the contract phase, I wanted to understand the positions we took and why we took them.

MY APPETITE TO LEARN WAS BORN OUT OF MY DESIRE TO EVENTUALLY HAVE AS MUCH CONTROL
OVER THE PROCESS AS POSSIBLE. I WAS ACTIVELY INVOLVED AND I KNEW WHAT I WANTED FROM DAY ONE.
IT WAS LIKE I WAS IN BUSINESS SCHOOL.
I TOOK THE PROCESS VERY SERIOUSLY BECAUSE MY PARENTS HAD DRILLED INTO MY HEAD THE NEED
TO BE PREPARED FOR LIFE AFTER BASKETBALL. THEY HAD SHOWN ME EXAMPLES OF PLAYERS
WHO MADE A LOT OF MONEY PLAYING THE GAME AND A FEW YEARS AFTER THEIR CAREERS ENDED
DIDN'T HAVE A THING. I GOT THE POINT.

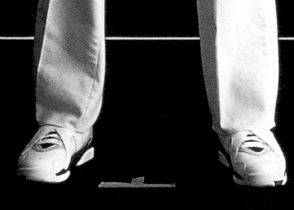

Even at the end of my career I was always
comparing myself to other players. I wanted to know where
I stood, how I matched up, what I needed to work on.
I always wanted to be sure I was doing everything I could to stay on top.
It never had anything to do with money or business.
The game is what mattered to me. In the early years I compared myself
to Magic and Larry. What could I do to elevate my game past theirs?

MOST VALUABLE PLAYER * LEADING SCORER * DEFENSIVE PLAYER

They were great all-around players,
but they were never known as great defenders.
I realized defense could be my way of separating myself from them.
I decided I wanted to be recognized as a player who could influence
the game at either end of the floor. The one thing people saw
in me that they didn't see in Magic or Larry was the athletic ability.

They had great talent, but in terms of raw athletic ability
I think I had a little more. To some extent I think it was
hard for people to believe anyone who jumped and dunked could
also be a complete player. But that's what I did at North Carolina
and that's what I was trying to do in the NBA.
After the 1987–88 season the critics had to say,
"This kid can have an influence at both ends of the court.

THE YEAR ✳ STEALS LEADER ✳ SLAM-DUNK CHAMPION ✳ ALL-STAR

He's not just a scorer." Now when they talked about Magic
and Larry they also had to talk about defense. I felt like I made the
separation, at least individually, to some extent that season.
But I knew I'd never completely be recognized
as their equal until we won championships.

I was wrong about the Charles Oa

Oakley was a tough rebounder and he gave us a physical presence against teams such as Detroit. He was young, hard working, and unselfish. He had every attribute you wanted in a teammate. Cartwright had been injured for years and he was on the back end of his career. I loved Charles like a brother, still do, and I hated to see him traded. I felt like we were giving away too many years trading for an older guy who couldn't stay healthy. I didn't know anything about Bill's personality. Would he stand up against the Pistons? I thought we needed the kind of toughness Charles gave us because we still were trying to break

I loved having Charles on the te

kley—Bill Cartwright trade in 1988.

through Detroit. But it turned out to be an important trade given where we were headed as a team. We struggled through the 1988–89 season trying to fit a low-post player into an offense that basically revolved around my game. That was still a year before Phil Jackson instituted the Triangle Offense. Bill didn't know how to adjust to a player like me and I didn't know how to adjust to him. Personally, we had our problems in the beginning. I had to learn how and where to deliver the ball to Bill. It took awhile before I started to appreciate what Bill gave us and how he could compensate for the loss of Charles.

am, but Bill made the difference.

BY THE START OF THE 1988—89 SEASON THE CHALLENGE WAS NO LONGER AS MUCH PHYSICAL
AS IT WAS MENTAL. I WAS PERCEIVED AS A GREAT PLAYER, BUT THE CRITICISM WAS STILL THE SAME:

THE BULLS WILL NEVER WIN A CHAMPIONSHIP WITH MICHAEL JORDAN LEADING THE LEAGUE IN SCORING.

SCORING CHAMPIONSHIPS		
Player	Scoring Titles	Scoring Titles in NBA Championship Year
Michael Jordan	10	6
George Mikan	3	2
Kareem Abdul-Jabbar	2	1
Joe Fulks	1	1
Wilt Chamberlain	7	0

They pointed to Wilt, Dominique Wilkins, Bob McAdoo, guys who scored a lot of points but played on teams that weren't nearly as successful as those players were individually. Kareem Abdul-Jabbar was the only player since George Mikan to lead the league in scoring and take his team to a championship. A non-center never had won both in the same season. History presented a great argument for those looking to criticize what I was doing on the floor. Because I was perceived as being more successful than the team, the perception held that I didn't make the players around me better. But I knew what I could do on the court. That's why the challenge became more mental. I had to incorporate my ability into a system that made the team better. Doug never really had a system because he relied on individual talent. In that sense, I needed the right players around me to make the team better. That started happening when Horace Grant and Scottie Pippen began developing and Bill became a low-post threat. But it didn't happen overnight. When Oakley left and Cartwright arrived, I knew I would have to rebound more. Later, when Scottie and Horace became starters, I knew I would have to find ways to get them into the offense. Doug tried everything including moving me to point guard late in the season. That was the first time all season everything started to click. We won 11 of 14 games during one stretch and I had 10 triple doubles in 11 games. I could see the whole floor and teams no longer could key on me defensively. For the first time in my career we had other scoring options and teams had to respect my teammates. But there was a lot of friction on the team, particularly between Doug and some of the younger players. Still, I knew we had taken a step forward. We lost all six games we played against Cleveland and all five against Detroit during the regular season. But by the time the playoffs started I really thought we could beat anybody.

TEAM IMPROVEMENT

1984-85	1985-86	1986-87	1987-88	1988-89
REGULAR SEASON	REGULAR SEASON	REGULAR SEASON	REGULAR SEASON	REGULAR SEASON
38-44	30-52	40-42	50-32	47-35
PLAYOFFS	PLAYOFFS	PLAYOFFS	PLAYOFFS	PLAYOFFS
1-3	0-3	0-3	4-6	9-8

THERE ARE PLAYS THAT STAND OUT IN YOUR MIND, THINGS YOU DID THAT WHEN YOU SEE THE REPLAY IT ALMOST SEEMS LIKE YOU'RE
I DON'T REMEMBER WHAT YEAR IT WAS BUT THE REPLAY WAS IN SLOW MOTION. IT LOOKED LIKE ONE OF THOSE APOLLO BLASTOFFS IN SLOW

"WHEN DOES JUMPIN

THAT'S HOW IT LOOKED TO ME. WHEN PEOPLE WOULD ASK
I ALWAYS SAID, "YES, FOR A LITTLE WHILE." BUT WHEN I

WATCHING SOMEONE ELSE IN YOUR BODY. I REMEMBER ONE DUNK EARLY IN MY CAREER THAT I SAW ON VIDEO A COUPLE YEARS AGO. MOTION. I JUST KEPT GOING UP. I KNEW I WAS WATCHING MYSELF, BUT I STILL COULDN'T BELIEVE HOW IT LOOKED. I REMEMBER THINKING,

IG BECOME FLYING?"

WHETHER I COULD FLY, ESPECIALLY WHEN I WAS YOUNGER, SAW THAT DUNK IT REALLY DID LOOK LIKE I WAS FLYING.

I never considered the negative consequence of missing the last shot in a game. I missed my share, but I always had complete confidence the ball was going in. As time went on and I had more success in those situations, I became more comfortable with the role. Even later in my career, I always thought of Coach Smith in tight games or in situations that demanded a game-winning shot. We had just called our last timeout in the NCAA Championship game against Georgetown in 1982. He

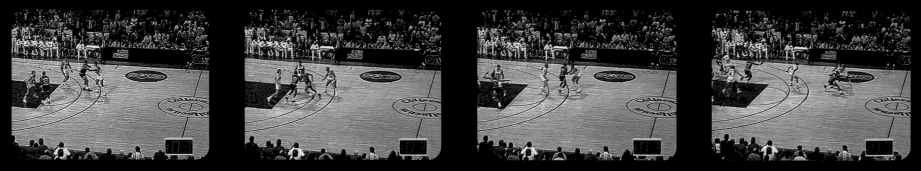

was getting ready to draw up a play for the final shot when he stopped. He looked up and said, "I love these games. They're fun because they make you think." There

we were in the heat of the battle and he's able to smile and laugh softly to himself. Then he said, "This is fun." It was like a kid playing a kid's game. Every time I

was in that situation, I thought about those words: "This is fun." That's exactly what I thought about in the timeout before the shot over Craig Ehlo that won Game 5 of the 1989 first-round playoff series against Cleveland. I had missed a free throw and a potential game-winner in Game 4 in Chicago and we ended up losing in overtime. That was about as low as I had ever felt in basketball. It reminded me of being cut from the varsity in high school. We had won 47 games during the reg-

GAME-WINNING SHOTS: (25) THE HARD WAY

◎ **Nov. 11, 1984 vs. Indiana**
12-foot jumper with four seconds left
Final Score: 118–116

◎ **Dec. 7, 1984 vs. New York**
18-foot jumper with five seconds left
Final Score: 95–93

◎ **March 26, 1985 vs. Indiana**
Two free throws with five seconds left
Final Score: 120–119

◎ **April 24, 1985 vs. Milwaukee**
Jumper from the corner with
22 seconds left to force Game 4 in
1985 first-round playoff series.
Final Score: 109–107

◎ **Oct. 25, 1985 vs. Cleveland**
Hits second of two free throws
for the victory
Final Score: 116–115

◎ **Nov. 11, 1986 vs. Atlanta**
Driving layup with nine seconds left
Final Score: 112–110

◎ **Nov. 21, 1986 vs. New York**
Scores final 18 Bulls points
including a running 18-footer
with one second left
Final Score: 101–99

◎ **Feb. 12, 1988 vs. Milwaukee**
Drops two free throws with two
seconds remaining
Final Score: 95–93

◎ **April 3, 1988 vs. Detroit**
Two free throws with four seconds left
Final Score: 112–110

◎ **April 15, 1988 vs. New Jersey**
Hits jumper with 20 seconds left
Final Score: 100–99

◎ **Feb. 16, 1989 vs. Milwaukee**
20 footer with one second remaining
Final Score: 117–116

◎ **May 7, 1989 vs. Cleveland**
"The Shot" over Craig Ehlo at the buzzer
to win the first-round playoff series
Final Score: 101–100

◎ **May 19, 1989 vs. New York**
Two free throws with four seconds left
Final Score: 113–111

ular season and we should have closed out Cleveland at home. So when the opportunity presented itself in Game 5, I had to find a way. The shot was all heart and determination. The entire series was built on those elements. Cleveland beat us 5–0 during the regular season and we were supposed to be swept. Utah in 1998 was supposed to do the same thing. They were supposed to beat us because we had a hard seven-game series against Indiana. It's a matter of accepting your position with

a determination to change that position. If you accept the expectations of others, especially negative expectations, then you never will change the outcome. I believed

no one could determine or dictate the result of a game I was playing. In Cleveland, none of us believed we were going to lose, despite the records. We could determine

the outcome. That was the attitude I had ever since I was cut from the varsity team in high school. That attitude became a part of me. I can't be successful without that approach. When I was in a situation where everyone knew I was going to take the last shot, I enjoyed looking in my opponent's face. They knew it, I knew it, the fans knew it. The challenge in that moment is making it happen.

◎ **May 27, 1989 vs. Detroit**
Pull-up jumper over Dennis Rodman
with three seconds left
Final Score: 99–97

◎ **Nov. 13, 1990 vs. Utah**
15-foot jumper over Thurl Bailey and Jeff
Malone at the buzzer
Final Score: 84–82

◎ **Jan. 22, 1992 vs. Charlotte**
Picks up loose ball, goes length
of the court, and is fouled on score
for three-point play
Final Score: 115–112

◎ **Nov. 11, 1992 vs. Detroit**
Drains long-range three-pointer
at the buzzer
Final Score: 98–96 (OT)

◎ **May 17, 1993 vs. Cleveland**
"The Shot—Part Two," a jumper over
Gerald Wilkins at the buzzer to win
Game 4 of the 1993 Eastern
Conference Semifinals
Final Score: 103–101

◎ **March 25, 1995 vs. Atlanta**
Brings the ball up court and hits jumper
over Steve Smith at buzzer
Final Score: 99–98

◎ **Feb. 11, 1997 vs. Charlotte**
Hits three-pointer at the buzzer
Final Score: 103–100

◎ **March 18, 1997 vs. Seattle**
Hits two free throws with
eight seconds left
Final Score: 89–87 (OT)

◎ **June 1, 1997 vs. Utah**
Hits three-pointer over Byron Russell
to win Game 1 of the 1997 NBA Finals
Final Score: 84–82

◎ **Feb. 13, 1998 vs. Atlanta**
Hits another winner at the buzzer
over Steve Smith
Final Score: 112–110

◎ **March 22, 1998 vs. Toronto**
Drains a fall-away jumper from
right wing with five seconds left.
Final Score: 102–100

◎ **June 14, 1998 vs. Utah**
Knocks down 17-foot jumper with
5.2 seconds left to clinch the
Bulls sixth championship
Final Score: 87–86

Patrick Ewing and I joke about it but he never has been able to overcome that defeat
in the 1982 NCAA Championship game. He has tried, but he never has been able to break through against me.
He never beat me head-to-head in a playoff series, either. He might have won some games in the
regular season, but when it mattered Patrick never got past me.

IT'S THE SAME WITH CHARLES BARKLEY, KARL MALONE, AND JOHN STOCKTON, TOO. THEY WERE MY PEERS IN MY TIME JUST AS MAGIC JOHNSON AND LARRY BIRD WERE THE GUYS I WAS TRYING TO GET PAST EARLY IN MY CAREER.

DO I FEEL SORRY FOR THEM?

NO.

I NEVER COULD FEEL SORRY FOR THEM BECAUSE THAT WOULD SHOW I HAD LOST
SOME OF THE EDGE I HAD AGAINST THEM. PATRICK AND I TALK ABOUT HOW OUR CAREERS
HAVE CROSSED OVER THE YEARS. BUT THERE'S NOTHING BUT LOVE BETWEEN THE TWO OF US.

HE'S A GREAT FRIEND.

HE CALLED ME AND ASKED ME ABOUT MY PLANS.
I TOLD HIM I WAS GOING TO RETIRE. HE SAID,

"YOU CAN'T RETIRE. YOU HAVE TO COME BACK. I'VE GOT TO BEAT YOU."

MAYBE ON THE GOLF COURSE.

etroit taught us how to maintain our cool and to play through situations without losing sight of our objective. Their game was to intimidate, to divide, and to conquer an otherwise united team by forcing players to react emotionally. The Pistons tried to get you to play angry, which meant you were playing out of control. All that pushing and shoving was their way of getting the minds of opposing players off the gameplan. That's what Dennis Rodman was all about. He would try to get

Jordan vs. The Jordan Rules

Instituted after 59-point performance in
112-110 Bulls victory at Detroit April 3, 1988

	vs. League		vs. Detroit	
	FG%	Scoring	FG%	Scoring
1988 Playoffs	53.1%	36.3	49.1%	27.4
1988-89	53.8%	32.5	44.9%	27.7
1989 Playoffs	51.0%	34.8	46.0%	29.7
1989-1990	52.6%	33.6	42.8%	26.0
1990 Playoffs	51.4%	36.7	46.7%	32.1

inside a player's head and take that player out of the game mentally. Once he had distorted the guy's thought process, the physical part was easy. Chuck Daly, who coached Detroit at the time, had his own plan for me. The Jordan Rules were a set of defensive principles the Pistons applied to stop me. As far as I could tell the plan involved running as many players as possible at me whenever I touched the ball and then hitting me as hard as possible every time I took a shot. Some rules.

IF YOU BOUGHT INTO THEIR TACTICS,

YOU WOULD BECOME VINDICTIVE BECAUSE OF ALL THE STUFF THEY WERE DOING TO YOU.

SO THEY FORCED US TO LEARN
HOW TO KEEP OUR COMPOSURE.

ONE MAJOR DIFFERENCE BETWEEN PHIL JACKSON AND DOUG COLLINS WAS THE ATMOSPHERE IN THE HUDDLE AND

ON THE BENCH IN CLOSE GAMES.

(W)ith Doug you could feel the tension, while Phil was poised at all times. Doug was more emotional. He wasn't afraid to show you exactly how he was feeling. As a player you connected with the atmosphere the coach created. With Phil it was like we were in harmony with each other in the heat of the battle. We were comfortable not only with each other but also with the situation no matter how difficult the moment. We were able to find peace amid the noise, and that allowed us to figure out our options, divine solutions, and be clear-headed enough to execute them. That's what Phil Jackson brought to the Chicago Bulls and that's what we all connected with. That's one of the reasons we became so successful for so long. And that's why we eventually cut the heart out of Detroit. That presence, that peace of mind, that connection between the team and the coach was more valuable than anyone possibly could know. But that was Phil. That was who he was at the core of his being. It wasn't contrived. The Zen Buddhist philosophy, the middle-road approach to life, Phil lived that philosophy every day and he brought elements of that philosophy to the team. He taught us to find peace within ourselves and to accept the challenges, whatever they may be at whatever moment they appear. It wasn't just an intellectual passing out information. We were able to see the embodiment of those thoughts every day. Phil lived by those principles. And nothing changed with all the success. Even as we won championships, Phil remained the same within the team.

2

IN THE YEARS BETWEEN 1989 AND 1993 I BECAME A MAN.

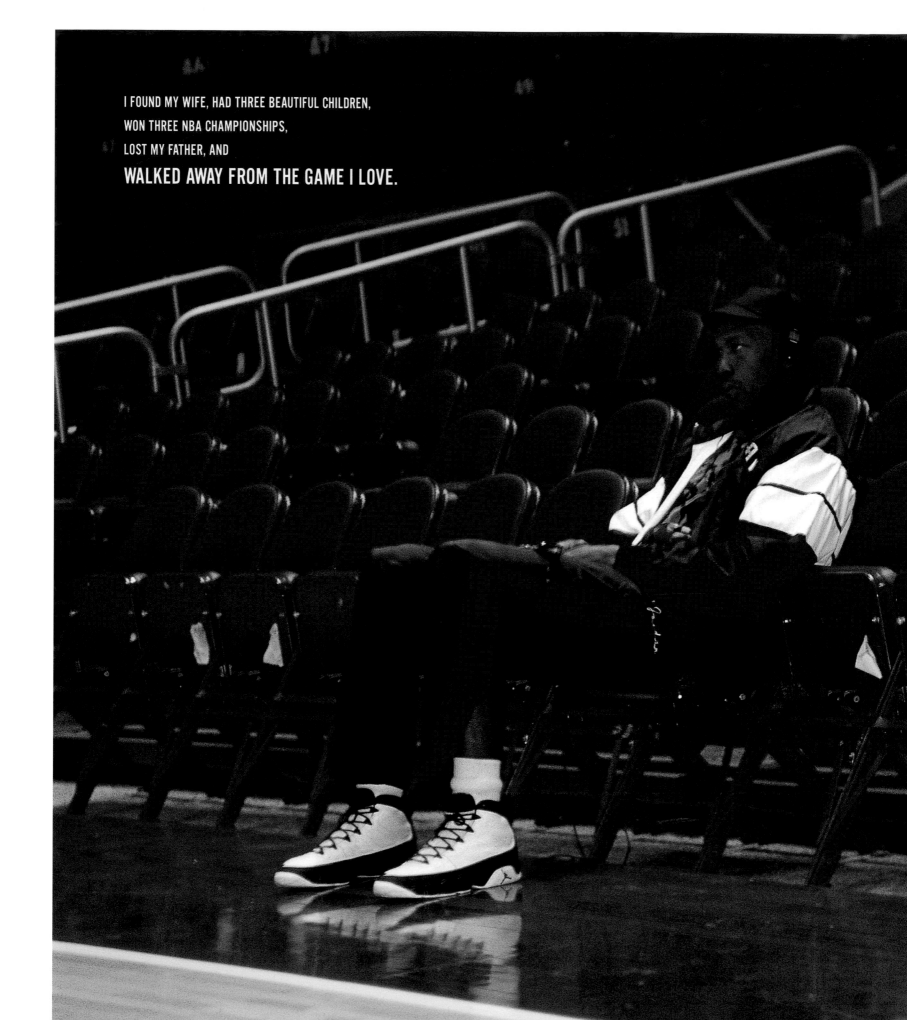

I FOUND MY WIFE, HAD THREE BEAUTIFUL CHILDREN,
WON THREE NBA CHAMPIONSHIPS,
LOST MY FATHER, AND
WALKED AWAY FROM THE GAME I LOVE.

IN THE SPAN OF FOUR YEARS,
FROM SEPTEMBER OF 1989 UNTIL SEPTEMBER OF 1993,
MY LIFE CHANGED IN WAYS I COULD NOT HAVE IMAGINED.

In some cases, particularly with the births of my children, the highs were higher than ever. But so too were the lows. I learned what it was like to be criticized, to have your life put under a magnifying glass for the purpose of exposing some deep dark secret or to find that one indiscretion that would knock me off the pedestal others had created for me. On the basketball court, I elevated my game to meet the demands of our team and my own expectations. The game began to become more mental than physical, the challenges more narrowly focused. Off the court, the balance and harmony created by the presence of my family got turned upside down with my father's passing. I had been playing a kid's game and leading a kid's life. By the time I retired from basketball in 1993, I was a man leading a man's life.

WHEN PHIL TOOK OVER BEFORE THE 1989–90 SEASON,
I FELT MY GAME CHANGING AND I REALLY DIDN'T HAVE ANY CONTROL OVER
WHAT WAS HAPPENING. FOR THE FIRST TIME WE HAD AN IDENTIFIABLE SYSTEM DESIGNED
TO INTEGRATE EVERYONE INTO THE OFFENSE.

IN THE BEGINNING
I FOUGHT THE TRIANGLE.

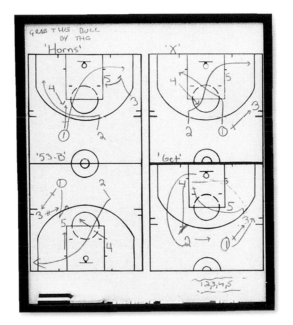

Ithought Phil believed all the talk about not being able to win a championship with me leading the league in scoring. I thought he went to that offense to take the ball out of my hands. For the first time since college, I wasn't the first option. The first option was to throw the ball inside to either Horace or Bill. I wasn't alone in fighting the system. Everyone hated it in the beginning because it was so difficult to operate. But Phil never backed off. He and Bulls assistant coach Tex Winter, who invented the system, forced the offense on us until we finally started to develop a rhythm within the system. I can't say it worked all the time, but at least it kept everybody occupied and involved. The Triangle allowed all of us to break down our defender before the rest of the defense realized what was happening. Because of all the movement involved in executing the offense, the system forced defenders to be honest. They couldn't double me as easily because I usually was moving without the ball. The offense was designed to make every player a scoring option. That's where Scottie, Bill, and a sidekick like John Paxson became so important. When Paxson's man started to become dishonest, boom, John would knock down a jump shot that would extend the defense even more. As a result, I had more room to operate. Detroit's "Jordan Rules" became less effective because I had too many options.

I ALWAYS HAD THE FADEAWAY BUT I DIDN'T HAVE TO USE IT EARLY IN MY CAREER BECAUSE I WENT ONE-ON-ONE AGAINST MY OPPONENT. I COULD FACE UP TO THAT PLAYER AND BREAK HIS DEFENSE DOWN WITH MY QUICKNESS. THE PISTONS CHANGED THE WAY I ATTACKED. THEY SAID, "WE'RE NOT GOING TO LET YOU ISOLATE, AND ANYTIME YOU START TO DRIVE WE'RE GOING TO CLOSE DOWN THE LANE AND WE'RE GOING TO BEAT YOU UP." THEY TRIED TO BEAT ON ME FROM THE SECOND I TOUCHED THE BALL ALL THE WAY THROUGH THE MOVE, ESPECIALLY IF I WAS GOING TO THE BASKET. THE PURPOSE OF THE TURNAROUND JUMP SHOT WAS TO AVOID GIVING DEFENDERS A CHANCE TO SEE ME IN FRONT OF THEM AND REACT. WHEN I GOT THE BALL ON THE BLOCK I WAS IN THE DANGER ZONE. I COULD REACT BEFORE THEY COULD SEND HELP. I DIDN'T HAVE THE BALL IN FRONT OF THEM SO THEY COULDN'T SEND PLAYERS AT ME. ✳ A YOUNG PLAYER FROM DUKE ASKED ME OVER THE SUMMER WHY EVERYBODY DIDN'T KNOW I WAS GOING TO BE A GREAT PLAYER BEFORE I BECAME ONE. COMING OUT OF HIGH SCHOOL EVERYONE IS INDI-VIDUALLY TALENTED, BUT NO ONE IS DEFENSIVELY FOCUSED. THERE AREN'T MANY HIGH SCHOOL KIDS THAT GET A COLLEGE SCHOLARSHIP ON DEFENSE. NOW YOU GO TO A GOOD SCHOOL, DUKE OR NORTH CAROLINA, WHERE THEY TEACH YOU THE FUNDAMENTALS. YOU PROBABLY CAN'T SCORE LIKE YOU DID IN HIGH SCHOOL, SO THEY TEACH YOU HOW TO DEVELOP OTHER PARTS OF YOUR GAME. YOU LEARN TO PLAY WITHIN A SYSTEM AND YOU'RE NOT AS SUCCESSFUL OFFENSIVELY AS YOU WERE AT THE HIGH SCHOOL LEVEL. THEN YOU LEAVE COLLEGE, WHICH IS LIKE LEAVING HOME. THEY HAVE BEEN TEACHING YOU EVERYTHING ABOUT THE GAME AND NOW YOU'RE OUT IN THE WORLD OF THE NBA. NOW YOU HAVE TO PUT EVERYTHING YOU'VE LEARNED IN 21 YEARS TO WORK. YOU HAVE TO LEARN HOW TO APPLY THAT KNOWLEDGE, BECAUSE AS A PROFESSIONAL YOU GET SOME OF THAT OLD INDIVIDUALITY BACK. THERE ARE NO ZONES, THE SHOT CLOCK IS 24 SECONDS, AND THE SYSTEMS AREN'T AS TIGHT AS THEY ARE IN COLLEGE. BUT YOU HAVE TO LEARN HOW TO APPLY INDIVIDUAL TALENTS IN GAME SITUATIONS THAT VARY FROM TEAM TO TEAM FOR 82 GAMES. IT SOUNDS LIKE AN OVERWHELMING CHALLENGE. IF YOU'RE A STUDENT OF THE GAME AND YOU'RE CONSTANTLY TRYING TO GET BETTER, YOU WON'T BE SATISFIED SIMPLY WITH REACHING THE HIGHEST LEVEL OF BASKETBALL. AS LONG AS I PLAYED THE GAME I WAS LEARNING. FOR ME, ESPECIALLY LATER IN MY CAREER, THE CHALLENGE AND THE LEARNING PROCESS WAS ALL MENTAL. THE PHYSICAL CHALLENGE WENT AWAY FOR ME A LONG TIME AGO. I PROVED I COULD TAKE OFF FROM THE FREE THROW LINE AND DUNK OR LEAD THE LEAGUE IN SCORING. AFTER THAT, THE CHALLENGES BECAME MORE AND MORE MENTAL FOR ME.

I KNEW WE HAD ALL THE PIECES TO THE PUZZLE IN 1990.

STILL, WE LOST 106–81 TO DETROIT
AT HOME IN THE MIDDLE
OF MARCH IN A KEY GAME.
I REMEMBER ISIAH THOMAS SAYING

"THE CENTRAL DIVISION
RACE IS OVER."

(A) ll I could think was, "Not yet. You have to be aware of the opposition before you make statements like that." Over the next six weeks we got to within two games, but we couldn't catch them. Whatever control they

Pistons and Knicks had figured the only way to throw me off my game was to throw me out of the air. I'd had enough. I wanted to start dishing out the punishment instead of taking it all the time. We came back from

The game at Cleveland, March 28, 1990, started out like any other game until I took a hard foul early from Hot Rod Williams. He knocked me to the court and I was down for a minute or two. As I was lying there I could hear the crowd cheering. I couldn't believe they would prefer to see me hurt if that helped them win a game. That wasn't good sportsmanship. Every athletic event I had ever been to when someone got hurt and got up people clapped. The fans were still loyal to their team, but they understood a player's well-being was more important than a basketball game. I was down on the floor and they were cheering. I looked over at Bulls trainer Mark Pfeil and said, "These people are about to pay for it." I got up, made my free throws, and it was like I was in a controlled rage from that point forward. Doug could see it because Doug kept giving me the ball. I was like a possessed man playing that game. I went to work. It didn't look like 69 points because I was scoring in the flow of the game. There were a couple of other games where I played with that kind of emotion. I had 49 against Detroit the first game after the 1985 All-Star Game. There were a few games where I played with

69

MICHAEL JORDAN—March 28, 1990—The Coliseum

MIN	FG	FGA	3PT	3PTA	FT	FTA	RB	AST	STL	PTS
50	23	37	2	6	21	23	18	6	4	69

a kind of controlled anger. The Jerry Stackhouse game in Philadelphia in 1996 is another good example. Stackhouse had said he played me one-on-one and he didn't think I was that good and that I just got all the favorable calls. That set me off. I had 44 after the third quarter and called off the dogs because we were so far ahead. LaBradford Smith gave me 37 points one night in Chicago. We played them at Washington the next night. I told him I'd get 37 by halftime of that game and ended up with 34 at half. There were a couple games against the Knicks when their coaches made a statement I didn't

agree with. During the 1989 playoffs I turned my ankle and Rick Pitino, who was the Knicks coach, went on TV and said he really didn't think I was hurt. I made sure it didn't look like I was hurt the next day and dropped 47 on him. Jeff Van Gundy did the same thing during the 1996 playoffs. He called me a con man and said I lulled opposing players to sleep by befriending them. That really irritated me. I gave him 44 points the next day and said, "Con that, little man." Everyone asked me what I said to Van Gundy after the game. And that's about as nice a translation as I can give you.

BEST OF THE BEST
TOP
10
HIGHEST SCORING GAMES OF CAREER
Regular Season

69	3/28/1990	@ Cleveland	117-113
64	1/16/1993	Orlando	124-128 (ot)
61	3/4/1987	@ Detroit	125-120 (ot)
61	4/16/1987	Atlanta	114-117
59	4/3/1988	@ Detroit	112-110
58	4/26/1987	New Jersey	128-113
57	12/23/1992	Washington	107-98
56	3/24/1987	Philadelphia	93-91
55	3/28/1995	@ New York	113-111
54	11/3/1989	Cleveland	119-124 (ot)

I HAVE USED VISUALIZATION TECHNIQUES FOR AS LONG AS I CAN REMEMBER. I ALWAYS VISUALIZED MY

SUCCESS. IT WASN'T UNTIL LATER IN MY CAREER THAT I REALIZED THE TECHNIQUE IS SOMETHING

MOST PEOPLE HAVE TO LEARN. I HAD BEEN PRACTICING THE PRINCIPLES NATURALLY MY ENTIRE

LIFE. I VISUALIZED HOW MANY POINTS I WAS GOING TO SCORE, HOW I WAS GOING TO SCORE THEM,

HOW I WAS GOING TO PLAY AND BREAK DOWN MY OPPONENT. IF I WAS PLAYING AGAINST A

SCORER LIKE REGGIE MILLER, I WOULD ENVISION HIS TENDENCIES,

HIS FAVORITE SPOTS ON THE FLOOR, HOW HE LIKED TO RECEIVE

THE BALL. IT'S LIKE I WOULD WATCH THIS LITTLE GAME UNFOLD IN

MY MIND. THEN I'D MAKE DECISIONS BASED ON WHAT I SAW. SHOULD

I ATTACK EARLY TO PUT HIM ON HIS HEELS? I HAD TO STOP HIM

VISUALIZATION

AS WELL AS SCORE ON HIM, SO I WOULD DEVISE A PLAN BASED ON WHAT I HAD VISUALIZED. I DIDN'T PAY TOO MUCH ATTEN-TION TO STATISTICS, SO I DIDN'T ALWAYS KNOW IF A GUY WAS SHOOTING WELL OR NOT. BUT I HAD SEEN EVERY PLAYER IN THE LEAGUE ENOUGH TO KNOW HIS PREFERENCES.

IT DIDN'T ALWAYS PLAY OUT EXACTLY HOW I SAW IT, BUT MOST OF THE TIME IT DID. THE PROCESS OF SEEING SUCCESS BEFORE IT HAPPENED PUT ME IN A POSITIVE FRAME OF MIND AND PREPARED ME TO PLAY THE GAME. ONCE THE GAME STARTED, I NEVER THOUGHT ABOUT WHAT WAS SUPPOSED TO HAPPEN. INSTINCTS TOOK OVER. BUT IN A WAY, I KNEW I ALREADY HAD SEEN SPECIFIC WAYS IN WHICH THE GAME COULD UNFOLD.

NO ONE EVER DEFINED THE REQUIREMENTS TO BE MOST VALUABLE PLAYER. IF THE CRITERIA WAS CLEAR, THEN THERE NEVER WOULD HAVE BEEN A QUESTION AS TO WHO SHOULD HAVE WON. SHOULD THE PLAYERS VOTE? SHOULD THE MEDIA? I DON'T KNOW THAT IT REALLY MATTERED BECAUSE IT WASN'T CLEAR WHO WAS THE BEST QUALIFIED. BEING NAMED MVP FIVE TIMES WAS A GREAT HONOR. BUT THE ONE AWARD THAT MEANT THE MOST TO ME DURING MY CAREER WAS BEING NAMED DEFENSIVE PLAYER OF THE YEAR IN 1988. BEFORE THAT YEAR NO ONE EVER HAD BEEN NAMED MOST VALUABLE PLAYER AND DEFENSIVE PLAYER OF THE YEAR, MUCH LESS LEAD THE LEAGUE IN SCORING AND STEALS. THAT AWARD MADE A STATEMENT ABOUT WHAT I WAS ABOUT. NOW I WASN'T JUST SEEN AS A SCORER. I SCORED MORE THAN 29,000 POINTS IN MY CAREER AND I HAVE THE SECOND-MOST STEALS IN HISTORY. THOSE ARE THE KIND OF STATISTICS THAT 20 YEARS FROM NOW WILL PROVIDE A BETTER UNDERSTANDING OF WHAT MICHAEL JORDAN WAS ALL ABOUT. IT WASN'T JUST AT THE OFFENSIVE END. IT WAS ALL FACETS OF THE GAME AND THAT IS SOMETHING I'M MOST PROUD OF BECAUSE IT SHOWS I HAD A WELL-ROUNDED GAME. TO BE NAMED DEFENSIVE PLAYER OF THE YEAR AS A SHOOTING GUARD, TO HAVE 200 STEALS AND 100 BLOCKS TWICE, I HAD TO BE THAT PRODUCTIVE TO CONVINCE PEOPLE I WAS MORE THAN AN OFFENSIVE WEAPON.

MY TROPHY ROOM. THE FLOOR CAME FROM THE OLD CHICAGO STADIUM.

AWARDS

- 1985 All-Rookie First Team
- 1985 Rookie of the Year
- 1985 All-NBA Second Team
- 1985 IBM Award, All-Around Contribution to Team's Success
- 1987 Slam-Dunk Champion
- 1987 All-NBA First Team
- 1987 Scoring Champion
- 1988 Most Valuable Player
- 1988 Defensive Player of the Year
- 1988 Slam-Dunk Champion
- 1988 All-Star Game Most Valuable Player
- 1988 All-NBA First Team
- 1988 Scoring Champion
- 1988 Steals Champion
- 1988 All-Defensive First Team
- 1989 All-NBA First Team
- 1989 All-Defensive First Team
- 1989 Scoring Champion
- 1989 IBM Award, All-Around Contribution to Team's Success
- 1990 All-NBA First Team
- 1990 All-Defensive First Team
- 1990 Scoring Champion
- 1990 Steals Champion
- 1991 Most Valuable Player
- 1991 Scoring Champion
- 1991 All-NBA First Team
- 1991 All-Defensive First Team
- 1991 NBA Finals Most Valuable Player
- 1992 Most Valuable Player
- 1992 Scoring Champion
- 1992 All-NBA First Team
- 1992 All-Defensive First Team
- 1992 NBA Finals Most Valuable Player
- 1993 Scoring Champion
- 1993 All-NBA First Team
- 1993 All-Defensive First Team
- 1993 Steals Champion
- 1993 NBA Finals Most Valuable Player
- 1996 Most Valuable Player
- 1996 Scoring Champion
- 1996 All-Star Game Most Valuable Player
- 1996 All-NBA First Team
- 1996 All-Defensive First Team
- 1996 NBA Finals Most Valuable Player
- 1997 Scoring Champion
- 1997 All-NBA First Team
- 1997 All-Defensive First Team
- 1997 NBA Finals Most Valuable Player
- 1998 Most Valuable Player
- 1998 Scoring Champion
- 1998 All-Star Game Most Valuable Player
- 1998 All-NBA First Team
- 1998 All-Defensive First Team
- 1998 NBA Finals Most Valuable Player

I LOVED PLAYING THERE.

Every night I had an opportunity to showcase my talents. I knew there would be someone on the floor

or in the crowd who wanted to know whether all the things they heard were true.

IS MICHAEL JORDAN REALLY THAT GOOD?

I looked at every game as an opportunity to show the world that, yes, it's true.

I took the same approach in practice. If a new player came to the Bulls I wanted him to know I earned everything that came my way.

Some nights I didn't get it done up to my expectations much less everyone else's. But I could accept that.

I didn't lose my mind because I wasn't able to please the crowd. There were certain nights I was going to be a normal player. But over the course of a season I wanted to be consistent, particularly on the road. That's what I strived for, a consistent level of excellence. On the road I was able to draw energy from the hostile environment. I knew the opposing team was more comfortable at home and that extra degree of difficulty presented a unique challenge. I'm quite sure another player might have seen my situation and considered the expectations a burden. But I looked forward to the challenge. In the playoffs everything went up another notch because the fans were even more hostile and the stakes were much higher. But I never considered the expectations or the demands stressful. Just the opposite. There was a purity, a simplicity to the challenge from individual players in their comfortable surroundings. It was right there in front of you. I always could respond to that kind of challenge.

There were three players the Bulls were looking at before the 1990–91 season.

Walter Davis, Danny Ainge, and Dennis Hopson

were all available and the team had enough salary cap room to bring one of them in.

I wanted Walter Davis

because I knew he still could score and he'd be able to take some of that pressure off me.

I always loved Walter's game and I knew he wouldn't be bothered by the Pistons' tactics.

But Walter's wife didn't want to move to Chicago. So Krause asked me about Ainge and Hopson.

I had a simple answer: Find out how each of them did against Detroit the last couple years and

get the guy who performed the best. But Krause had his mind made up before he even talked to me.

He wanted Hopson.

Now I knew Dennis Hopson wasn't the kind of guy we could count on against Detroit.

I could see fear in his eyes every time we played New Jersey, which is where Hopson had played.

Why not Ainge?

I knew Danny wouldn't back down from the Pistons and he had played enough with Larry Bird and

the Celtics to understand what it took to win. But Krause thought Hopson could be a "franchise-type" player

and that he just needed a new outlook because things hadn't gone well for him in New Jersey.

WELL, THEY DIDN'T EXACTLY GO GREAT IN CHICAGO, EITHER.

When we learned how to play through their tactics without losing focus, we became the good guys because we played the game the way it was supposed to be played. They couldn't pull us down to their level and they certainly couldn't intimidate us. When that happened, when we broke through and swept them four straight in the 1991 Eastern Conference Finals, the leaders of that team showed their true colors. They acted like a bunch of spoiled brats who didn't get their way. They lost a lot of respect by walking off the floor and not shaking our hands.

NO ONE REMEMBERS JOE DUMARS, JOHN SALLEY, AND VINNIE JOHNSON COMING OVER AND CONGRATULATING US AFTER THE GAME.

All anyone remembers is their leaders, Isiah Thomas, Bill Laimbeer, and Mark Aguirre, walking right past our bench as the final seconds ticked off. They weren't sportsmen. They either didn't understand or didn't care about sportsmanship. That's not how the game should be played. You have the obligation to demonstrate good sportsmanship. That's the American way.

BY THE TIME WE WENT THROUGH THE PISTONS
THE PUBLIC SAW HOW DETROIT PLAYED.
I'M SURE THERE WERE DIE-HARD DETROIT FANS WHO THOUGHT
THE WAY THE PISTONS PLAYED WAS FINE, BUT EVERYONE ELSE HAD SEEN ENOUGH TO KNOW
WHAT THEY WERE ABOUT. EVEN AFTER TWO CHAMPIONSHIPS,

FANS BEGAN TO SEE THEM AS BULLIES

TRYING TO DISTORT THE GAME WITH THAT BEAT-EM-UP AND KNOCK-EM-DOWN APPROACH.

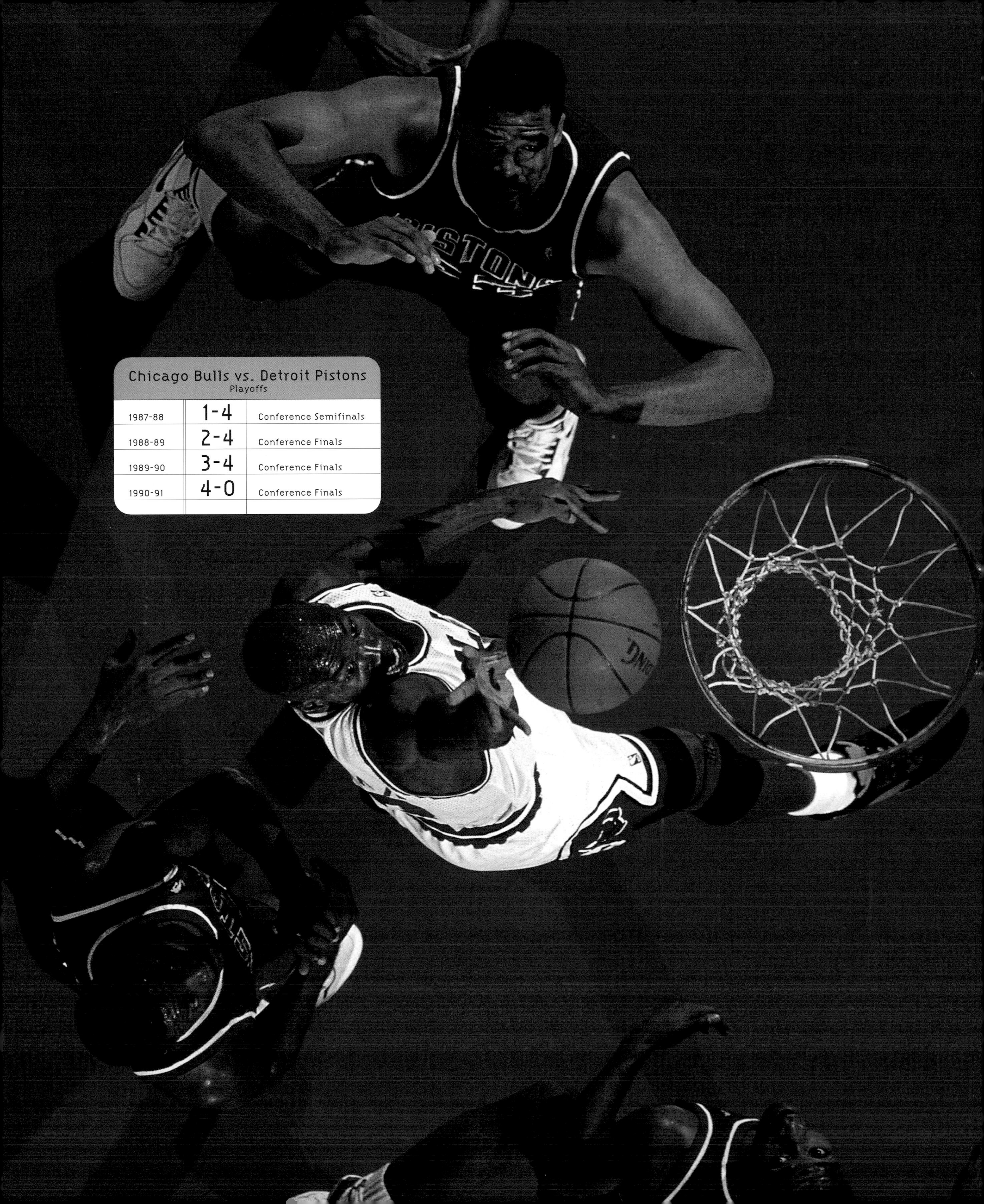

Chicago Bulls vs. Detroit Pistons		
Playoffs		
1987-88	1-4	Conference Semifinals
1988-89	2-4	Conference Finals
1989-90	3-4	Conference Finals
1990-91	4-0	Conference Finals

JORDAN		MAGIC
5	G	5
220	MIN	228
113	FGA	58
63	FGM	25
33	FTA	41
28	FTM	39
33	RB	40
37	AST	62
14	STL	6
7	BLK	0
156	PTS	93
31.2	AVG	18.6
36	HI	22

first

I HAD WON SCORING TITLES AND MOST VALUABLE PLAYER AWARDS, BUT THE ONLY WAY I WAS GOING TO BREAK INTO THE MAGIC JOHNSON—LARRY BIRD CLASS WAS TO WIN CHAMPIONSHIPS.

There was no way I was going to get into their circle without winning a championship when at least one of them was still on top. Magic and Larry had been the kings of the 1980s in terms of championships. In 1991, the challenge was right there in front of me. Magic was considered the consummate team player, the guy that made everyone around him better. I wasn't perceived as a player who made everyone better and I knew I wouldn't be until we won a title. Patrick Ewing, Charles Barkley, Karl Malone, and John Stockton? I didn't want Magic to retire before we won a championship just like they didn't want me to retire before they could win one. They wanted to go through me just like I wanted to go through Magic. Beating Magic added credibility to that first title.

THAT'S WHY OUR FIRST CHAMPIONSHIP WAS A LITTLE SWEETER.

Barkley, Malone, Ewing, and Stockton, they don't want their championship to be tarnished by my absence. Look at Houston. The Rockets won back-to-back titles and they have to listen to people talk about whether or not they would have won anything if I had been playing. It's not fair, but that's the way it is. And it was no different for me. That's why it was so important to go through Magic and the Lakers for our first championship. By going through the Lakers there was nothing anyone could say. If both of them had been gone by the time we started winning championships I'm sure there would have been talk about how I hadn't been able to beat Magic and Larry in their prime. Maybe not after we won six championships, but at the time? Yes.

MAGIC'S AGENT CALLED DAVID FALK AND TOLD HIM TO CALL ME RIGHT AWAY. I WAS DRIVING HOME FROM PRACTICE WHEN DAVID CALLED, FRANTIC ABOUT HIS CONVERSATION. HE SAID MAGIC HAD SOMETHING VERY IMPORTANT TO TALK TO ME ABOUT AND I HAD TO CALL HIM RIGHT AWAY. SO I DID. I GOT AHOLD OF MAGIC AND SAID, "WHAT'S UP?"

HE TOLD ME HE WAS HIV-POSITIVE

AND THAT HE WAS GOING TO ANNOUNCE HIS RETIREMENT

IN A PRESS CONFERENCE ABOUT AN HOUR LATER.

I WAS STUNNED.

I COULDN'T EVEN DRIVE. I PULLED OFF TO THE SIDE OF THE ROAD

AND JUST LISTENED. I DIDN'T FULLY UNDERSTAND WHAT HE WAS SAYING AT FIRST.

I KNEW OF AIDS, BUT I WASN'T SURE WHAT HIV WAS EXACTLY.

HE EXPLAINED THE SITUATION, WHAT IT MEANT, AND WHAT HE WAS GOING TO DO.

I COULDN'T BELIEVE IT. EVERYTHING HE SAID WAS OPTIMISTIC.

HE SAID HE WAS GOING TO BEAT IT AND THAT EVERYTHING WOULD BE FINE.

IF THAT WOULD HAVE BEEN ME, I WOULDN'T HAVE BEEN ABLE TO TALK TO ANYONE.

I WOULDN'T HAVE WANTED TO TALK TO ANYONE.

I CAN'T IMAGINE CALLING ME UP AND CALMLY EXPLAINING THE SITUATION AND REMAINING OPTIMISTIC.

I WOULDN'T HAVE BEEN ABLE TO SPEAK.

HOW MANY OTHER HIGH-PROFILE PEOPLE COULD HAVE STOOD UP,
FACED THE MUSIC, AND THEN GONE TO WORK ON THE PROBLEM?

MY ROOTS JUST KEPT GETTING DEEPER.

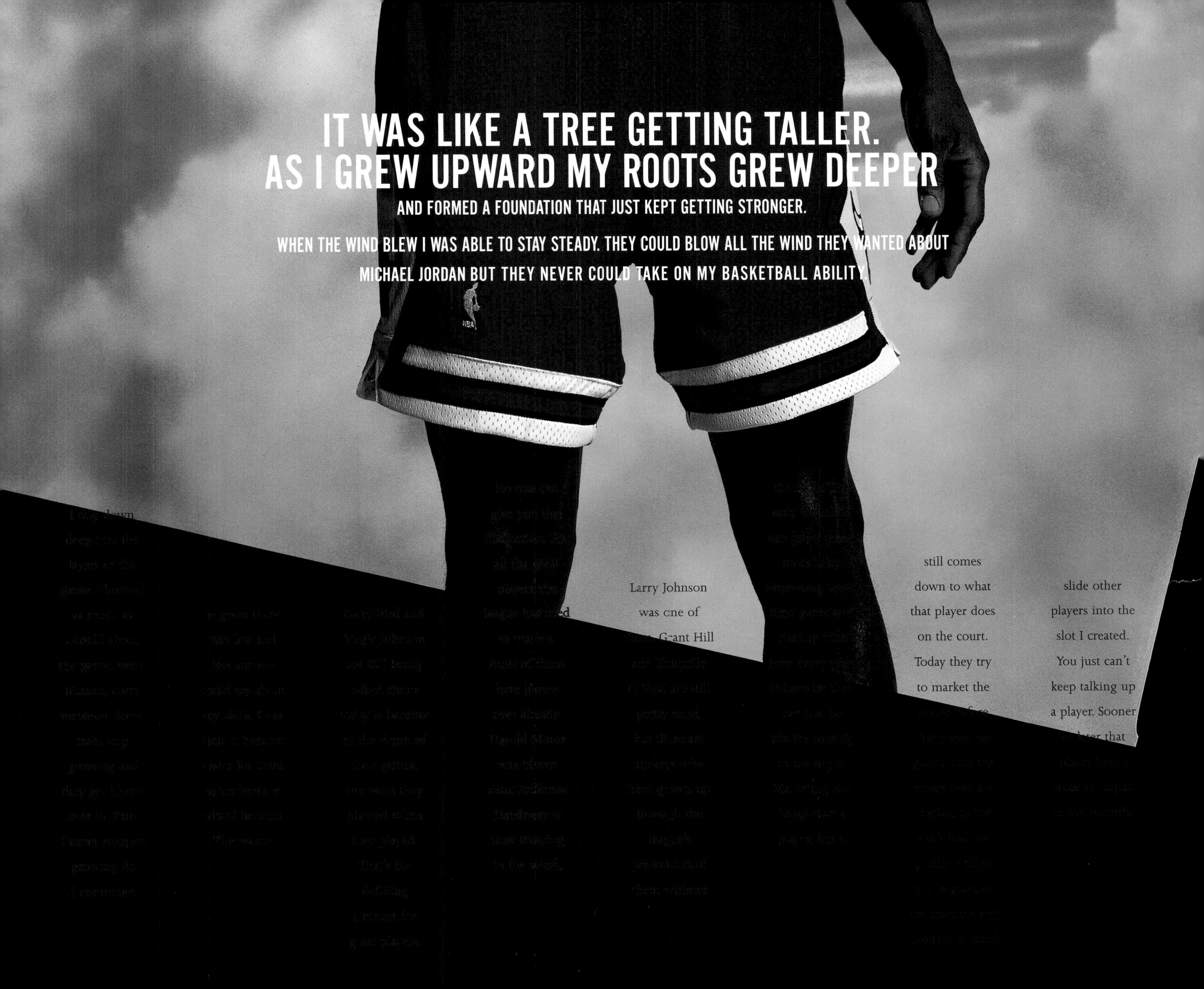

IT WAS LIKE A TREE GETTING TALLER.
AS I GREW UPWARD MY ROOTS GREW DEEPER

AND FORMED A FOUNDATION THAT JUST KEPT GETTING STRONGER.

WHEN THE WIND BLEW I WAS ABLE TO STAY STEADY. THEY COULD BLOW ALL THE WIND THEY WANTED ABOUT

MICHAEL JORDAN BUT THEY NEVER COULD TAKE ON MY BASKETBALL ABILITY.

still comes

down to what

that player does

on the court.

Today they try

to market the

keep talking up

a player. Sooner

slide other

players into the

slot I created.

You just can't

Larry Johnson

was one of

Grant Hill

I admit, I made some mistakes.

Until the 1991–92 season there really hadn't been much written or said negatively about me. After we won the first championship there wasn't anything anyone could really say about my basketball anymore so they started looking at me personally. I admit, I made some mistakes. They weren't huge mistakes, not the kind that change your life. But I also stood up and faced the fire. The gambling stories were situations I put myself in and I was responsible for my actions. But the way I dealt with those situations, particularly the gambling issue, was human. I made a mistake and I faced the heat. To some degree I think people started seeing me as more like them, more of a person with

problems and issues. The way I had been perceived up to that point really wasn't reality. It was a difficult time, but I grew up. I was no longer just playing a game that paid me a lot of money and earned me the adoration of millions

of fans. It wasn't that simple anymore, and in some ways it wasn't that pure, either. I was experiencing basketball as a business, on and off the court. I didn't make any serious mistakes. I didn't have trouble with alcohol, drugs

or anything like that, but I wasn't some kind of perfect person that floated above life's day-to-day issues.

JORDAN	1992 NBA FINALS COMPARISON	CLYDE
6	G	6
254	MIN	238
154	FGA	118
81	FGM	48
46	FTA	56
41	FTM	50
29	RB	47
39	AST	32
10	STL	8
2	BLK	6
215	PTS	149
35.8	AVG	24.8
46	HI	32

THE 1992 FINALS AGAINST PORTLAND WERE SUPPOSED TO DETERMINE
THE DIFFERENCE BETWEEN CLYDE DREXLER AND MYSELF.

second

To that point Clyde had been seen as a version of me, not necessarily a better version. So I'm sure that presented a challenge for him. But I took that discussion the same way. I wanted people to know there was a distinct difference, just as there was when I played against Magic, Charles, and other big-name players. I used the first championship against Magic to gain credibility. He was the guy on top at the time and I had to beat him to earn my place. By the time we played Portland I was the guy on top because we were the defending champions. Clyde wanted to use me the same way I used Magic. Later in my career, players wanted to go through the

Chicago Bulls because it would legitimize the championship. I thought there was a difference, a real difference. It was similar to the 1998 All-Star game when Kobe Bryant was trying to make his mark against me. It's not something you announce but it's a challenge that simmers right below the surface. I was trying to break Clyde down by using all the facets of my game to say, "Don't even think about it." Besides, I had studied Clyde. I knew that if he hit his first three shots there wasn't a shot on the floor he wouldn't take. Interestingly, he was more dangerous if he missed the first three because he would focus on other aspects of the game. He would look to go to the basket and pick up a foul. He did have that great first step. I'm pretty sure he tried to push me to my left as well because that was my weaker hand. Portland played us tough but repeating was never about the physical difficulty involved in getting the job done. Winning two or three titles in a row was always more mental than physical. The only exception to that notion was 1998, which was a very physically draining year with all the injuries and the lack of understanding by some players about what it took to win three straight.

IF THERE IS ONE PLAYER I WOULD HAVE LIKED TO PLAY AGAINST IN HIS PRIME IT WOULD HAVE BEEN

Jerry West.

	Jerry WEST	Michael JORDAN
SEASONS	14	13
ALL-NBA FIRST TEAM	10	10
ALL-DEFENSIVE FIRST TEAM*	4	9
MOST VALUABLE PLAYER	0	5
SCORING AVERAGE	27.0	31.5
ALL-STAR GAMES	14	12
FG PERCENTAGES	.474	.505
FT PERCENTAGES	.814	.838
REBOUNDS	5.8	6.3
ASSISTS	6.7	5.4
PLAYOFF SCORING AVERAGES	29.1	33.4

*Team started in 1968-69, West's 9th season

He was a great clutch shooter, he could jump, he was tough, and he was quick.

I would have liked to test myself against him at his best.

HOW WOULD I HAVE DONE?

We'll never know. From what I have read about Jerry and from what others have told me,

he played the game a lot like I did. He was a great scorer, but he also played good defense. Could he have stopped me? I don't think so.

COULD I HAVE STOPPED HIM?

I don't know. But it would have been a great matchup.

HOW WOULD I HAVE DONE AGAINST ME?

It might sound strange, but I've often wondered how I would have done against myself.

How would I have attacked at the offensive end? What would I have done defensively? There were some cracks,

but I'm never going to tell anybody what they were. I think I could have done some things defensively,

but I also know I would have come up with ways to counter those tactics offensively. The difference would have been mental.

I wouldn't be able to out-think myself. The heart would be the same, the work ethic just as strong. I wouldn't have had an edge,

at least not the edge I had against everyone else. Some nights it was being smarter, some nights stronger, and some nights just tougher.

I could jump over certain guys, get by others, and later take most of them into the post. If I couldn't throw off their rhythm defensively,

then I would attack them at the offensive end. I felt like I had a lot of weapons and not all of them were physical in nature. But against myself?

I know myself too well. I can't say I would have won because that means I would have lost. It would have been fun to watch, though.

THE NEW YORK KNICKS TEAMS OF THE EARLY 1970S WERE VERY SIMILAR IN MAKEUP TO OUR FIRST THREE CHAMPIONSHIP TEAMS. EVEN THE COACHES, RED HOLZMAN AND PHIL, WERE SIMILAR IN THE WAY THEY FOCUSED ON TEAM DEFENSE AND DEALT WITH PLAYERS. THE KNICKS HAD WILLIS REED, DAVE DEBUSSCHERE, BILL BRADLEY, AND WALT FRAZIER. BOTH TEAMS DISTRIBUTED THE BALL SELFLESSLY AND WORKED AS A UNIT TO MAKE THINGS HAPPEN AT THE DEFENSIVE END. WE HAD BILL CARTWRIGHT, JOHN PAXSON, SCOTTIE, AND ME. THE FIRST TWO CHAMPIONSHIP SEASONS WE WERE CONNECTED JUST LIKE THOSE KNICKS TEAMS. BILL WAS LIKE REED, PAXSON WAS SMART LIKE BRADLEY, PIPPEN DID A LITTLE OF EVERYTHING LIKE DEBUSSCHERE, AND I PLAYED BOTH ENDS LIKE FRAZIER. LIKE OUR BULLS TEAMS, THOSE KNICKS COULD HAVE WON IN ANY ERA. THE GAME MAY CHANGE AND PLAYERS MAY BECOME MORE SKILLED, BUT THE KIND OF PLAYERS

DAVE DEBUSSCHERE   WALT FRAZIER   WILLIS REED   PHIL JACKSON   BILL BRADLEY

WHO WIN CHAMPIONSHIPS NEVER CHANGE. GIVE ME GUYS WITH HEART, BRAINS, AND STRONG FUNDAMENTALS. NO MATTER WHAT HAPPENS IN THE GAME OF BASKETBALL, THOSE ELEMENTS WILL ALWAYS DETERMINE SUCCESS AND FAILURE. LOOK AROUND THE NBA. WERE THE BULLS ALWAYS THE MOST TALENTED TEAM? NEVER. OUR LAST THREE CHAMPIONSHIP TEAMS WERE HELD TOGETHER BY A COMMON BOND. WE KNEW HOW TO PLAY THE GAME AND WE KNEW HOW TO WIN.

INDIVIDUAL ABILITY PUT US IN POSITION, BUT EVERYTHING ELSE IS WHAT PUT US OVER THE TOP. JUST LIKE THOSE KNICKS TEAMS, WE HAD LEARNED HOW TO BREAK DOWN AN OPPONENT AND EXECUTE WHEN THE GAME WAS ON THE LINE. THAT'S HEART. AND THAT COMES FROM WITHIN. GIVE ME FOUR GUYS WITH GREAT HEART AND I'LL BEAT FIVE GUYS WITH GREAT POTENTIAL ANY TIME.

LEADING UP TO THE 1992 BARCELONA OLYMPICS, THERE WERE SOME BUSINESS CONCERNS A NUMBER OF US HAD
ABOUT REEBOK'S PRESENCE ON THE USA BASKETBALL WARMUPS.
I WAS ASSURED EVERYTHING WOULD BE RESOLVED
BY THE TIME THE GAMES STARTED, SO I SIGNED ON TO PLAY.

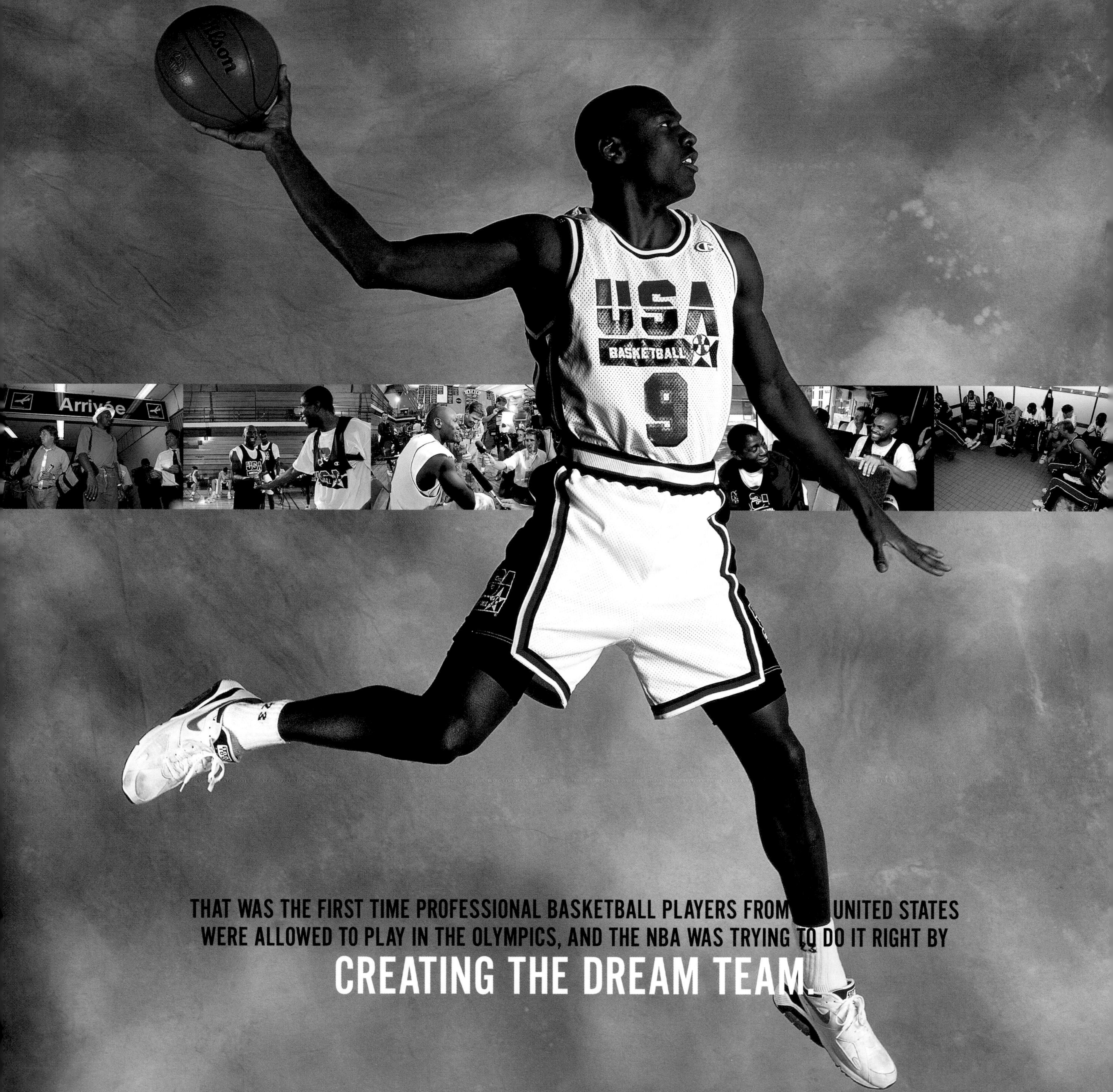

THAT WAS THE FIRST TIME PROFESSIONAL BASKETBALL PLAYERS FROM THE UNITED STATES
WERE ALLOWED TO PLAY IN THE OLYMPICS, AND THE NBA WAS TRYING TO DO IT RIGHT BY
CREATING THE DREAM TEAM.

I HAD WON A GOLD MEDAL IN THE 1984 GAMES,

SO MY FIRST THOUGHT WAS TO ALLOW SOMEONE ELSE TO HAVE THE OPPORTUNITY.

But the opportunity to spend time with Larry Bird, Magic Johnson, Charles Barkley, and some of the other guys appealed to me. We knew the games themselves wouldn't be that difficult. The only other issue involved my relationship with Nike and Reebok's sponsorship of USA Basketball. I knew I couldn't back out of the Olympics after I had agreed to go because that would have been un-American. I had committed to play for my country and I wasn't going to pull out over a logo, despite my loyalties.

Still, I didn't know how I would handle the medal ceremony. I wasn't about to stand up there in front of the world wearing a Reebok product. When it came time to receive the gold medal, we were told anyone who refused to wear the warmup wouldn't be allowed on the stand. Finally, about 20 minutes before the medal ceremony, I came up with an idea. Charles Barkley, Scottie Pippen, and I decided to go into the stands and collect American flags.

WHO COULD ARGUE WITH THE FLAG?

WE GOT ONLY FOUR OF THEM, BUT EACH OF US DRAPED ONE OVER THE LOGO.

We might have been just as successful if Phil had been more of a company man, but I don't think our chemistry would have been as good. We wouldn't have felt the same level of obligation. I'm not sure some of the other players would have gone that extra mile. Phil dealt with us every day and he understood what our objectives were as a unit. He understood, from one day to the next, what was happening with us individually and collectively. He was the only one who knew. No one else in the organization had that kind of insight. How could they?

Phil knew our strengths, he knew our weaknesses. Theoretically, if you had a dispute with the coach, a player or that player's agent could go to management and complain. But we had no dispute with Phil because we knew his primary objective was to put together the best team. We all had the same objective, and Phil knew more about the individual parts than anyone.

Guys like Jud Buechler relied upon Jerry Krause for a contract, so they had to stay in Jerry's good graces. But those guys also relied on me, Scottie, and Phil. I had a voice and I had options, so players kind of lived through me when it came to dealing with management. I never minced words with Jerry. I let him know exactly how I felt right to his face.

As players, we drew a line between the team and the rest of the organization. We knew Phil wanted exactly what we wanted. And we responded. I think our respect for Phil and the general lack of respect for Krause is what helped pull the Chicago Bulls apart. Krause lied about little things my children would lie about. And for what purpose? To show who's boss? We had one of the most successful teams in the history of team sports and this guy is running around playing games with his own troops? I never understood all that and I never will.

The relationship between Phil and Krause had been ruined before the 1997–98 season started. Phil told Jerry, "Stop feeling as though you've made all the right decisions. I'm just as much a reason for this team being successful as you are." That rubbed Krause the wrong way. He might have come from a different era, but I think Krause understood the depth of Phil's impact on the team. He knew why the players liked Phil and he knew why we busted our butts for Phil. But Krause wanted to be the reason we played hard. He wanted to be the guy the players respected and talked to. When Phil signed his last contract, Krause told him, "I don't care if you go 82–0. You're not coming back next season." That's why Phil knew it was over from the beginning of the season.

ALL THAT TALK ABOUT BRINGING HIM BACK FOR ONE MORE YEAR AND KEEPING THE TEAM TOGETHER AFTER OUR SIXTH CHAMPIONSHIP WAS PUBLIC RELATIONS.
MANAGEMENT KNEW PHIL WASN'T COMING BACK AND PHIL KNEW MANAGEMENT DIDN'T WANT HIM BACK.

WHAT WOULD YOU DO? HOW COULD YOU RELY ON A GUY LIKE JERRY KRAUSE?

HE WOULDN'T TELL YOU IF THE SUN WAS OUT. BESIDES, PLAYERS NEVER HAD A DAY-TO-DAY RELATIONSHIP WITH HIM. JERRY RESENTED PHIL BECAUSE THE COACH AND PLAYERS HAD A MUTUAL RESPECT.

WE ALL EARNED THAT RESPECT FROM ONE ANOTHER.

WE KNEW PHIL WAS REAL BECAUSE WE COULD SEE HIM EVERY DAY. THERE WAS NO WAY MANAGEMENT COULD HAVE FORCED PHIL TO BE SOMEONE ELSE. HE HAD A DIFFERENT CONNECTION.
HE UNDERSTOOD MANAGEMENT'S VIEWS, BUT PHIL ALSO BELIEVED IN TREATING PLAYERS AS INDIVIDUALS WITHIN THE GROUP. IN A SENSE, THAT WAS HIS GIFT TO US.

PHIL WAS SPECIAL.
EVEN JERRY KRAUSE KNOWS THAT.

From the moment training camp started in 1992 I knew we had lost something. The team was no longer connected, and Horace Grant was the first one to break that connection. Horace couldn't accept his level on the team. Scottie and I had gone right from our second championship to the Barcelona Olympics. Our window for getting rest and bouncing back for the 1992–93 season was closing quickly by the time we returned from Spain. Phil understood how we felt and allowed us to practice once a day during the first week of camp. Horace, who had an entire summer off, had to practice twice a day with everyone else and he rebelled. He felt there was a double standard and that he had earned the right to be treated like Scottie and me. At the same time, some people started whispering in Horace's ear. He was a follower, not a leader, so Horace listened to people tell him how great he was and how I received freedoms and special attention. My relationship with Horace was never the same. Horace wanted to be at a certain level and Phil wouldn't put him there. So

Horace got angry and started creating a wedge within the team. There were things leaked to the media that I said in private or on the team bus. That's when the atmosphere within the team became tense. We were not friends at that time. On the court we did our jobs, but away from the game the harmony Phil had created was disrupted. There were guys I could see whispering to a reporter and the next day there's a quote from an anonymous source. I knew exactly who was saying what and so did everyone else on the team. How can you play with someone when you are afraid of saying something to them in private? I felt I was past all that childish stuff and I didn't want to deal with it anymore. Phil knew what was going on, but he had his own problems with B.J. Armstrong. B.J. was part of the new era of player. He wanted all his buddies to know he could average 20 points a night. But our system didn't allow a point guard to score like that. The system had been established and had been proven effective by the veterans. All we needed B.J. to do was step in and fill a role. We needed a point guard who got us into the system because the system worked. For a while I was able to deflect a lot of the friction between Phil and B.J. because I could talk to B.J. and I liked him. But he would look at John Paxson and think, "I'm quicker, I can get down the lane faster." What B.J. didn't see was John's savvy. I'm pretty sure if you ask B.J. now he realizes the system was perfect for him, too.

WE ALL HAD TO SUPPRESS OUR
EGOS
FOR THE SYSTEM.

THERE WAS A GREATER GOOD, BUT SOME OF THOSE GUYS DIDN'T UNDERSTAND THE CONCEPT.

J uanita and I were married before the 1989–90 season in the Little White Chapel in Las Vegas in front of a few friends. There was a reason for me getting married and having chil- dren. That experience of being a husband and a father provided a balance and a focus away from basketball. I could have gotten myself in trouble, I don't know what kind of trouble, but if I had been single, playing basketball, and making a lot of money, I could have made some wrong decisions. That's why I think our lives unfolded the way they did for a reason. When my first son was born, I felt like I became a man in a sense. There was a new level of maturity. Now I was responsible for that child and for the

During my mother's pregnancy with me, my mother's mother died unexpectedly.

The doctors made my mother stay in bed because they were worried about a miscarriage. According to my father,

there was a near miscarriage and there was some question as to whether I would make it or not.

I was born with a nose bleed and my parents were worried that there was something wrong with me.

Later on, when I was a baby, I fell behind my parents' bed and almost suffocated.

Then, when I was about two years old I picked up two wires next to a car my father was working on.

It had been raining and again, according to my father, the shock sent me flying about three feet.

There were a lot of things that happened even as I got older that could have changed everything.

I mean, my girlfriend got swept away in a flood and drowned when we were in college.

Another time, I was swimming with a friend when both of us got pulled into the ocean by a strong undertow.

I was able to get free and make it back to land. He never made it back.

HOW CAN YOU SAY THERE ISN'T A PLAN FOR ALL OF US?

mother of that child. Not tomorrow or the next day, but every minute of every day. I couldn't think selfishly anymore. There continue to be sacrifices based on the commitment I have to my family. But it has always been good for me.

It provided balance at a time when my life easily could have been out of balance. During that time they didn't know me as anything but Daddy. They didn't know anything about Michael Jordan the superstar basketball player

who did all kinds of endorsement deals. I was a father and a husband. They wouldn't have allowed me to be anything else. That was fine with me.

BY 1992 I
WAS BEGINNING
TO FEEL LIKE
A FISH IN
A FISHBOWL.

(M)Y LIFE WAS CHANGING AND THE WAY I WAS PERCEIVED WAS CHANGING, TOO. I WAS A FATHER AND A HUSBAND AT HOME, BUT EVERYWHERE ELSE I WAS MICHAEL JORDAN. AND IT SEEMED LIKE EVERYONE HAD AN IDEA OF WHAT THAT MEANT EXCEPT ME. EARLY IN MY CAREER I REALLY COULDN'T GET A SENSE OF WHO I WAS FROM THE FAN'S PERSPECTIVE. I DIDN'T FEEL AS FAMOUS AS PEOPLE SAID I WAS. I WAS SO FOCUSED ON THE GAME THAT I DIDN'T HAVE TIME TO STEP BACK AND CONSIDER MY LIFE IN THE CONTEXT OF EVERYONE ELSE. TO SOME DEGREE, I THINK THAT'S WHY I WAS SO WELL RECEIVED. I WASN'T ACTING. I WASN'T TRYING TO BE SOMETHING I WASN'T. I ALWAYS FELT COMFORTABLE IN THE SPOTLIGHT BECAUSE I WAS JUST BEING MYSELF.

✦ WITH MY PERSONALITY AND THE WAY I WAS RAISED, IT WOULD HAVE BEEN IMPOSSIBLE TO BE SOMETHING ELSE. MY PARENTS NEVER WOULD HAVE ALLOWED ME TO GET AWAY WITH SOME KIND OF ACT. I NEVER CONSIDERED MYSELF BETTER THAN ANYONE ELSE, NOT EVEN ON THE BASKETBALL COURT. I WANTED TO GET TO THE TOP AND I HAD A PRETTY GOOD IDEA OF WHAT IT TOOK. ✦ BUT LIFE ON A PEDESTAL CAN BE LONELY EVEN WITH A SUPPORTIVE FAMILY. WE WERE WINNING, I WAS PLAYING WELL, AND EVERYONE WAS SAFE. BUT I STARTED TO FEEL THE ATTENTION TAKE ON A DIFFERENT TONE. NO ONE WAS CRITICIZING MY BASKETBALL ANYMORE, SO THEY STARTED GOING AFTER ME PERSONALLY. I KNEW THAT TIME WOULD COME. IT ALWAYS DOES. IN A WAY, THAT'S THE BEAUTY OF AMERICA. WE HAVE THE FREEDOM TO BUILD PEOPLE UP AND TEAR THEM DOWN. EVERYONE CAN HAVE THEIR OWN OPINION AND I RESPECT THAT. ✦ BY THE BEGINNING OF THE 1992–93 SEASON, I WAS TIRED, PHYSICALLY AND MENTALLY. I HAD PLAYED FOR ALMOST TWO YEARS STRAIGHT, THERE HAD BEEN ONE MINOR CONTROVERSY AFTER ANOTHER, AND THE COHESIVE UNIT PHIL JACKSON HAD CREATED WAS STARTING TO COME APART. I COULD SEE THE EFFECT SUCCESS WAS HAVING ON CERTAIN PEOPLE. I KNEW THE NEXT 12 MONTHS WOULD BE DIFFICULT. BUT I HAD NO IDEA HOW HARD THEY WOULD BE AND JUST HOW MUCH MY LIFE WOULD CHANGE. ✦

I DIDN'T **PRACTICE** ZEN OR SIT IN A ROOM **AND MEDITATE.**

But Phil provided each of us with something we could incorporate into our lives. He didn't force-feed us, he just provided options. He presented the

thoughts intelligently. You could say there was some wisdom in his approach. He would appear to direct a thought or idea to the entire team, but usu-

ally the message was meant for an individual player. If you were that player, you got the message even though it was delivered to the entire group. That

was one of Phil's gifts, his ability to talk to us individually within the collective. It's what tied us all together. ☯ I realized early on that some of the

practices Phil spoke about I had been doing innately my entire life. For example, Phil brought in a sports psychologist to talk about getting into the

zone. Well, I had been there before so I understood the concept. I understood the rhythm of the moment and how the game starts flowing toward you.

I just couldn't comprehend how to get myself in the zone consistently. He provided methods and practices

designed to get us into the zone all the time. To achieve that level of awareness and understanding

really involves a level of perfection. I'm still not sure we are meant to understand how to think in

a manner that allows a player to spend an entire 48 min- utes in the zone. I relied upon game situations to find that

rhythm. But all these concepts gave me something to think about, to challenge myself with mentally. Sometimes it was hard to find a challenge phys-

ically, especially when I came back from baseball. But I have always been in tune with my body. When we first started meditating during stretching

before practice, I thought it was crazy. I'm closing one eye and keeping the other eye open to see what other fool is doing this besides me. Eventually

I became more accepting because I could see everyone making an effort. I opened my mind to meditation and Phil's teachings. My mind still travels a

little bit, but Phil taught us to concentrate on breathing to bring the mind back to center. There are certain times when I incorporate those thoughts

I'm sure no one noticed, but Dean Smith came up to Chicago  for a playoff game in 1993. We had talked all season about me

leaving the game. Up to that point he never had seen me play an NBA game in person. After a long talk in April, he asked if

AS EARLY AS THE 1992 OLYMPICS

this was the end and I told him, "Yes, it is." I needed a change because I no longer had the motivation that had carried me to that point in my career. I

I KNEW THE NEXT SEASON

would talk to Coach Smith every other week. I still do. We would talk about life, the family, what was happening with the team, how I was feeling men-

WOULD BE MY LAST. I HAD TALKED IT OVER

tally and physically. As the season progressed I knew he could sense my desire to leave. He never once tried to talk me out of it. He just wanted to under-

WITH MY FATHER AND HE KNEW I WAS

stand where I was mentally and how I had come to that decision. He said, "It has been a great run, you've accomplished a lot, and you have had a lot of

MENTALLY DRAINED. I NEEDED A BREAK AND

pressure. You probably do need a break." He always took that approach. He never tried to change a person's mind. Even when I was coming out of school,

I CONSIDERED LEAVING AFTER OUR

Dean never tried to talk me into staying despite the fact my leaving was going to have an impact on his program. He knew I was getting mentally ex-

SECOND CHAMPIONSHIP. THE ONLY REASON

hausted. We had won back-to-back titles, my time between seasons had been eliminated by the Olympics, and people were starting to pick away at me

I CAME BACK WAS TO WIN

personally. There were also a lot of things happening with the team that told me it was time to make a change. Everyone enjoyed being on top of the hill

A THIRD STRAIGHT CHAMPIONSHIP,

but they were starting to take shortcuts. It became such an unbelievable burden to constantly answer the critics, questions about Horace's contract, and all

WHICH WAS SOMETHING NEITHER

the sniping that was taking place between players. I didn't want any long good-byes and I certainly didn't want a season-long ceremony. By the time the

LARRY NOR MAGIC HAD DONE.

1993 playoffs started I had made up my mind. It was the perfect time. I knew it, my father knew it, and Dean knew it. No one else had a clue.

IF YOU PRACTICE THE WAY YOU PLAY, THERE SHOULDN'T BE ANY DIFFERENCE.
THAT'S WHY I PRACTICED SO HARD.

I WANTED TO BE PREPARED FOR THE GAME.

I PRACTICED HARD ENOUGH THAT THE GAMES WERE OFTEN EASIER. THAT'S EXACTLY WHAT I WAS TRYING TO ACHIEVE.
NO ONE CAN TURN IT ON WITHOUT PREPARING THEMSELVES IN PRACTICE. I HAD TO PRACTICE AS HARD AS I COULD SO ANYTHING WAS POSSIBLE ONCE THE GAME STARTED.
I LOVED THE COMPETITION OF PRACTICE. I GOT THAT FROM NORTH CAROLINA, WHERE COACH SMITH WOULD MAKE EVERY DRILL COMPETITIVE.
THAT GROWS ON YOU, SO EVERYTHING WE DID IN PRACTICE BECAME COMPETITIVE,
I TOOK PRIDE IN THE WAY I PRACTICED.

The fourth quarter of a basketball game changes the dynamics of the game for players. My focus would become clearer while other players lost their focus as the pressure mounted. A lot of times I was able to dominate in the fourth quarter because as I channeled myself into the game, my opponent was doing just the opposite, which doubled the impact of my attack. As the momentum starts to turn, the first thought for most players is a negative one. I never went into the fourth quarter of a game thinking we couldn't win. If I ever let a negative thought slip in, then I might as well have sat down. As long as I felt we could win, then believe me, brother, we are going to have an opportunity to win. Going into Game 6 of the 1998 Finals against Utah we went into the fourth quarter down three points. That was nothing. And it was nothing even with one of our key players out. My whole thought process was always, "We're going to win this game. I don't know how, but I believe we are going to win." It didn't matter whether we were down 4 points or 24 points. I always felt things would work out. During the 1997–98 season I built toward the fourth quarter because I was conserving energy early in the game. My game had always been to go all out for 48 minutes. Now I was conserving myself for the last 12 minutes.

third

PLAYING PHOENIX
AND CHARLES BARKLEY IN THE 1993 FINALS
WAS LIKE PLAYING AGAINST YOUR LITTLE BROTHER
AND KNOWING YOU'RE WELL-EQUIPPED.

YOUR LITTLE BROTHER MIGHT BEAT YOU
ONE OR TWO OUT OF SEVEN, BUT YOU KNOW
HE'S GOING TO GET BEAT IN THE END.
THE SUNS DIDN'T KNOW HOW TO WIN.
THEY KNEW HOW TO COMPETE,
BUT THEY DIDN'T KNOW HOW TO WIN.
THERE IS A DIFFERENCE.

1992 NBA FINALS COMPARISON

JORDAN		BARKLEY
6	G	6
274	MIN	277
199	FGA	126
101	FGM	60
49	FTA	56
34	FTM	42
51	RB	78
38	AST	33
10	STL	7
4	BLK	3
246	PTS	164
41.0	AVG	27.3
55	HI	42

MY FATHER'S DEATH ENDED ONE OF THE MOST SUCCESSFUL AND DIFFICULT PERIODS OF MY LIFE.

HE WAS MY BEST FRIEND AND HE KNEW EVERYTHING ABOUT ME.

HE KNEW THINGS THAT WERE GOING TO HAPPEN TO ME LONG BEFORE THEY HAPPENED. THE LIGHT SIDE OF MY PERSONALITY COMES FROM MY FATHER.

HE WAS A PEOPLE PERSON AND HE HAD A GREAT SENSE OF HUMOR. HE TAUGHT ME A LOT ABOUT LIFE,

AND ONE OF THOSE LESSONS WAS THAT EVERYTHING HAPPENS FOR A REASON.

That's why I was able to remain positive about life, my life, after my father's death. I look at that experience as God's way of telling me it was time to stand up and make decisions by myself. I no longer had the support and guidance of my father to fall back on. It was my time to become more mature in my approach to life. Everything I had done to that point, from basketball to business, I passed by my parents. I valued their opinion and to some extent I felt I needed their guidance. When he died I realized I had to start making those decisions independent of everyone else. I could still ask for advice and I would listen, but the responsibility was mine alone. I had to make the kind of decisions men make and I had to make them for myself without that shoulder to lean on. That doesn't mean he's not here with me at every moment. I can feel him. I know he's with me. I have all the life lessons and teachings he provided me in the 30 years I was around him. And I have his voice, his presence.

I know he's watching. I know how he's reacting to my success, the way my children are growing and how my life with Juanita has grown. So I look back at that period and his death as a test. But I also know I'll be taking that test for the rest of my life.

NO SMOKING

A COUPLE WEEKS AFTER OUR THIRD CHAMPIONSHIP I KNEW I WAS THROUGH. JERRY REINSDORF AND DAVID FALK TALKED ME INTO TAKING THE SUMMER TO THINK ABOUT WHAT I WANTED TO DO. BUT I KNEW MY FATHER'S DEATH AND EVERYTHING THAT FOLLOWED, THE ATTACKS ON ME AND MY FAMILY, THE SUGGESTION THAT I WAS SOMEHOW TO BLAME OR THAT MY GAMBLING PLAYED A ROLE, ONLY HELPED TO CONFIRM WHAT I KNEW MONTHS BEFORE. I NEEDED A BREAK. IN EARLY SEPTEMBER I MET WITH PHIL IN HIS OFFICE AT THE BERTO CENTER. I HAD BEEN IN THERE MANY TIMES BEFORE AND I KNEW I WOULDN'T BE IN THERE TOO MANY MORE TIMES IN THE FUTURE. I DIDN'T TAKE A LOT OF TIME.

I JUST ASKED HIM TO GIVE ME A REASON TO KEEP PLAYING.

Phil looked at me for a second or two and then talked about how I had a God-given gift and that I had a responsibility to use that gift for the benefit of others. I said I understood and that I agreed with his reasoning. But at some point in time I was going to retire anyway. What difference did it make if that time was now or two years from now? My gift would be taken away sooner or later, whether I liked it or not. Age and the simple passage of time would see to that. Phil looked at me and tried to make another point or two, but at that moment I knew what I was going to do. He just couldn't come up with a good enough reason for me to continue playing. And I didn't have one, either.

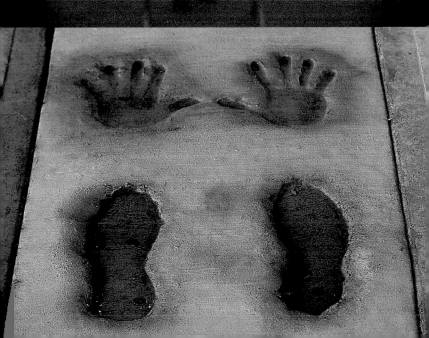

MICHAEL JORDAN

CHICAGO BULLS
1984 — 1993

The best there ever was. The best there ever will be.

3

IT WAS LIKE BEING A KID AGAIN.

(M)y father and I talked about baseball all the time because of what Bo Jackson and Deion Sanders were doing. He always had an idea about me playing baseball because he had started me in the game when I was growing up. I started getting invitations to play a game or two for minor league teams in the early 1990s. Muggsy Bogues and Del Curry had played a little bit with a team in North Carolina, so my father said, "Why don't you give it a try?" But I never had enough time in the offseason, and besides, I hadn't accomplished everything I wanted to accomplish in basketball. But I knew I'd give it a shot at some point. No one even knew we were having these conversations much less that I was serious about stepping away from the game of basketball. By the summer of 1992 I was ready to commit the entire summer to baseball. The Dream Team and the

I WAS THINKING ABOUT LEAVING BASKETBALL FOR BASEBALL AS FAR BACK AS 1991.

1992 Barcelona Olympics put my baseball plans on hold. Still, I didn't know for sure I was going to play baseball when I retired. I didn't know whether I'd have the opportunity to play. I went to Jerry Reinsdorf and told him it was something I wanted to pursue. He knew of my interest in the game, so he wasn't caught completely off guard. Neither one of us wanted to make a spectacle of my desire to play, so I started working out privately with Bill Melton, a well-known former White Sox player, and the team's trainer, Herm Schneider. After about eight weeks the news started to leak out and I told the world. I always considered myself a great all-around athlete and I believed I could do anything if I set my mind to it. I was serious about making the White Sox team.

I WAS SWINGING A 34-OUNCE BAT 300 TO 400 TIMES A DAY. I HAD BLISTERS ALL ACROSS MY HANDS EVEN WITH BATTING GLOVES.

HRNIAK, THE WHITE SOX HITTING COACH. I'D HIT WITH WALT FOR AN HOUR OR TWO, THEN GO THROUGH THE ENTIRE

IF ANYONE DIDN'T THINK I WAS SERIOUS
THE BLOOD DRIPPING OFF MY HANDS

THERE IS SO MUCH GOING ON IN THE COURSE OF A BASEBALL GAME THAT THE AVERAGE FAN NEVER SEES. HITTING SITUATIONS, PITCH COUNTS, WHEN AND HOW TO LOOK

THROWN AT ME. I PUT PRESSURE ON MYSELF BECAUSE I WANTED TO SUCCEED. BUT THE BEAUTY OF IT ALL WAS THAT NO ONE KNEW WHAT

BASEBALL. I HAD TO BUILD MYSELF UP FROM MY FINGERTIPS TO MY SHOULDERS.

WHEN WE GOT DOWN TO FLORIDA AND SPRING TRAINING, I WOULD BE THERE AT 6 O'CLOCK EVERY MORNING TO WORK WITH WALT PRACTICE AND FINISH THE DAY BACK WITH WALT. THAT WAS MY ROUTINE EVERY DAY OF SPRING TRAINING IN 1994.

IT WAS BECAUSE THEY COULD NOT SEE OR THOSE 6 A.M. BATTING SESSIONS.

FOR A SLIDER, A CURVEBALL AND FASTBALL, TWO-SEAMERS AND FOUR-SEAMERS, GETTING LEADS, READING A PITCHER FROM FIRST BASE, SLIDING. EVERYTHING WAS WOULD HAPPEN. NOT JERRY REINSDORF, NOT WHITE SOX GENERAL MANAGER RON SCHUELER, NO ONE KNEW WHETHER I WOULD SUCCEED.

HOW WOULD I DESCRIBE MY BASEBALL EXPERIENCE?

I WOULD DESCRIBE IT NOW THE SAME WAY I DESCRIBED IT THEN. EVERY MOMENT WAS A WARM ONE. I REMEMBER LOOKING UP IN THE SKY FROM TIME TO TIME AND BEING AMAZED AT HOW MUCH MY LIFE HAD CHANGED. I HAD NO FEAR. JUST A WARM FEELING. I CAN'T DESCRIBE THE SENSE EXACTLY, BUT NOW IT SEEMS LIKE I WAS LIVING A DREAM. MAYBE IT WAS THE PRESENCE OF MY FATHER THAT MADE THOSE MOMENTS SO WARM. I THOUGHT ABOUT HIM ALL THE TIME. AND I KNEW HE WAS THERE. IT WAS ALMOST LIKE WE WERE TOTALLY CONNECTED DURING THAT TIME.

The White Sox sent me to the Double A team in Birmingham in the Southern League. It turned out to be one of the best times of my life. I was learning, experiencing the game, and at the same time I was teaching the younger guys how to handle certain situations. They wanted to know everything about me and I wanted to know everything they knew about baseball. We were helping one another out in that way. I made sure we had a nicer bus, the team had to upgrade the living conditions on the road for security reasons, and when we went out to eat most of the time it was my treat. I was just happy to be a part of the team. There were a lot of things that felt good. The camaraderie was unbelievable compared to the NBA. We did things in groups, little things like going to dinner. Everything was purer, more genuine. Even the relationships had a purity and innocence to them. I wouldn't change anything about that experience.

I REALLY DIDN'T PAY MUCH ATTENTION TO BASKETBALL DURING BASEBALL. I NEVER THOUGHT I WOULD COME BACK, EITHER. I COULD SEE IMPROVEMENT AND I WAS STARTING TO BECOME COMFORTABLE WITH THE GAME. I HIT .202 AT BIRMINGHAM BUT I HIT .259 THE LAST MONTH AND PLAYED WELL IN THE ARIZONA WINTER LEAGUE. THERE WERE ONLY FIVE OTHER PLAYERS WHO HAD 50 RBI AND 30 STOLEN BASES IN THE SOUTHERN LEAGUE IN 1994, AND BY THE END OF THE SEASON I WAS FINDING MY POWER. BUT WHEN THE BASEBALL STRIKE STARTED I FELT LIKE I HAD BEEN PUT IN A BOX. I TOLD SCHUELER I DIDN'T WANT TO BE USED TO DRAW FANS INTO SPRING TRAINING GAMES. I DIDN'T WANT ANY PART OF CROSS-ING A PICKET LINE. THEY PUT ME IN A DIFFICULT SITUATION ANYWAY. I HAD OPTIONS BUT THE YOUNGER GUYS DIDN'T KNOW WHAT TO DO. THEY WERE COMING TO ME FOR ADVICE. SHOULD THEY REFUSE TO PLAY IN THE GAMES AND RISK BEING BLACK-BALLED BY MANAGEMENT, OR SHOULD THEY PLAY AND RISK BEING TARGETED BY THE PLAYERS? I FELT SORRY FOR THEM AND I DIDN'T KNOW WHAT TO SAY. WHEN THE WHITE SOX PUT ME IN THE SAME SITUATION I DECIDED TO WALK AWAY INSTEAD OF HELPING THE OWNERS.

$$45 \div 2 = 22.5$$

WHEN I CAME BACK I DIDN'T WANT TO PLAY WITH THE LAST NUMBER MY FATHER HAD SEEN ME WEAR.

BECAUSE HE WASN'T AROUND,

I THOUGHT OF MY RETURN AS A NEW BEGINNING.

THE REASON I CHOSE 45 WAS BECAUSE IT HAD BEEN MY NUMBER IN HIGH SCHOOL. MY BROTHER LARRY AND I PLAYED ON THE SAME TEAM WHEN I WAS A JUNIOR. HE WORE 45 AS A SOPHOMORE AND THAT WAS MY NUMBER. WHEN I GOT TO THE VARSITY, LARRY WAS WEARING 45 SO I CHOSE HALF OF THAT NUMBER, 22 1/2, WHICH WAS HOW I ENDED UP WITH 23. I WORE 45 IN BASEBALL BECAUSE THAT WAS THE NUMBER I STARTED WITH IN BASEBALL AS A KID.

I WORE THE NUMBER 9 IN THE OLYMPICS BECAUSE IT WAS FOUR AND FIVE ADDED TOGETHER. SO WHEN I CAME BACK I THOUGHT 45 WAS PERFECT BECAUSE I DID HAVE AN ASSOCIATION WITH THE NUMBER. BAD LUCK. IT DIDN'T TAKE ME LONG TO CHANGE BACK TO 23. IT WAS A PART OF ME, BUT NOT IN THE PROFESSIONAL BASKETBALL ENVIRONMENT.

$$\begin{array}{r} 4 \\ +5 \\ \hline 9 \end{array}$$

The first time everything clicked was my third game back against the Knicks in New York. I dropped a double nickel on them. I was still physically prepared to play baseball at that point. That game was strictly off talent. My game up to that point was up and down. You knew physically I wasn't ready to play because I couldn't consistently do my job. The guys hadn't seen me for a while so I think they forgot how I played. They let John Starks guard me one-on-one and they didn't double team. I was bigger than John and I could turn around and shoot over him all night long. They let me get into that zone. I think the fact the game was in Madison Square Garden had something to do with my performance. I always wanted to play well in New York because it's a basketball mecca.

DOUBLE NICKEL

WE GOT KNOCKED OUT OF THE 1995 PLAYOFFS BY ORLANDO
AND I KNEW I HAD A LOT OF WORK TO DO. I TOLD DAVID FALK
THERE WAS NO WAY I WOULD DO THE MOVIE "SPACE JAM" UNLESS I WAS ABLE TO WORK OUT
AND PLAY ON THE WARNER BROS. LOT.

There was no way I could stay out there for eight weeks after getting knocked out of the playoffs and being criticized for coming back. I said, "David, I need the work. I have got to practice. I need to play." He says, "What if we can create a working environment for you on the set that allows you to still do the movie?" I said, "Show me." So they built this state-of-the-art gymnasium that covered an entire parking lot. It had air-conditioning, stereo system, card tables, seats, lights, every conceivable weight-lifting machine, everything I needed. I would go over to the gym at lunch to lift weights and then return from about 7:00 to 9:30 every night to play. There was never a camera in the place. Reggie Miller and Chris Mills were there every single day. Charles Oakley came out and played, Magic came out the last day, Tim Hardaway, Dennis Rodman, all the UCLA players, Tracy Murray was there every day, Lamond Murray, Reggie Theus, Jawann Howard, Larry Johnson, Rod Strickland, Grant Hill, all kinds of guys came into town. The games were great. Oakley took over the middle and played just like he did during the season. Reggie and Eddie Jones went at it pretty good. I knew why these guys showed up. They wanted to learn and to try to get a feel for the way I played. I knew their strategy. But they didn't know I was doing the same. I always felt like I could learn faster than other people. So they were helping me just like I was helping them. I could feel it coming back pretty quickly.

72

I COULDN'T WAIT FOR THE 1995–96 SEASON TO START. I KNEW MY GAME HAD COME BACK WITH ALL THE WORK I PUT IN OVER THE SUMMER. I FELT LIKE A KID COMING OUT OF COLLEGE WITH SOMETHING TO PROVE. THE CONSENSUS WAS THAT I HAD LOST A STEP. BUT THERE WAS NO STOPPING US THAT SEASON. WE GOT OFF TO A GREAT START. WE WON 18 IN A ROW AT ONE POINT AND WERE ROLLING. WE HAD A SWAGGER ABOUT OURSELVES BECAUSE WE WERE DOMINATING. THEY KNEW WHAT WE WERE RUNNING, BUT WE JUST PICKED OPPOSING TEAMS APART. EVERYBODY ON THAT TEAM

10:39

WAS DEDICATED TO PLAYING THEIR ROLE BECAUSE MOST OF THEM HAD SOMETHING TO PROVE. NOT EVERYONE HAD WON A CHAMPIONSHIP. DENNIS RODMAN HAD WON IN DETROIT, BUT HE HAD TO PROVE HE COULD BE SOMETHING OTHER THAN A DISRUPTIVE INFLUENCE. OUR APPROACH THAT SEASON WAS RIGHT IN TUNE WITH MY ATTITUDE, WHICH WAS TO WIN AND BE DOMINANT IN THE PROCESS. 72 AND 10? IN THIS ERA WITH 29 TEAMS? INCREDIBLE. THAT WAS THE BEST RHYTHM ANY BULLS TEAM I PLAYED FOR HAD FOR AN ENTIRE SEASON.

THERE'S NOTHING EASY ABOUT

I know some players think they could do what I did if they had the kind of freedom I had. But they don't even have a basic understanding of what it takes to be that consistent over the course of an 82-game season. Before the 1997–98 season, Penny Hardaway told me he was going to win the scoring title and average 40 points a game. Shaquille O'Neal was gone and Hardaway figured he would have all the opportunities. He was serious, too. Do you know how hard it is to average 40 points? That's 10 points a quarter, every quarter of every game. And that's just your average. Now, if you don't score at least 10, then you have to score even more later.

You have to do that while the defense is completely focused on stopping you from scoring. That means you have to fight off double teams, get to the line, and knock down at least 80 percent of your free throws. All those things have to happen every single night. Scoring like I do doesn't happen because a situation changes or a player decides to be more aggressive. You have to study the game, find opportunities. The opportunities you find one night might not be there the next. You have to figure out ways to beat virtually every one

SUNDAY	
Games	Avg. Points
83	32.6

MONDAY	
Games	Avg. Points
68	30.7

TUESDAY	
Games	Avg. Points
185	31.2

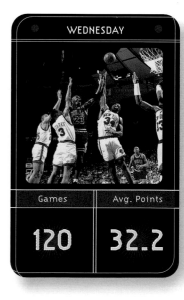

WEDNESDAY	
Games	Avg. Points
120	32.2

LEADING THE NBA IN SCORING.

of your opponents because you can be darn sure that if you're scoring that many points every one of your opponents is going to make a point of shutting you down. You have to be aggressive at all times mentally, then pick and choose when to attack physically. These kids don't understand that. They don't have

any understanding of the mental aspect necessary to score 40 points even one night.

You have to be able to adjust constantly. Do you come out at the beginning attacking to distort the entire game to your advantage? Do you try to get everyone else involved so they become a threat

and open the floor for you? I haven't even talked about what you have to do at the defensive end to get easy baskets. Steals, blocked shots, break-aways, all those situations play into a 32-point night. At this stage of their careers, guys such as Hardaway and Grant Hill are getting points strictly off phys-

ical talent. Now let's move to the playoffs, where you're playing the same team as many as seven times. The adjustments have to come quicker, sometimes between plays. And you have to do all these things with the objective of winning the game. I don't think any of them are ready for that.

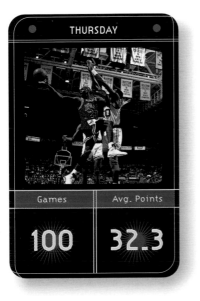

THURSDAY	
Games	Avg. Points
100	32.3

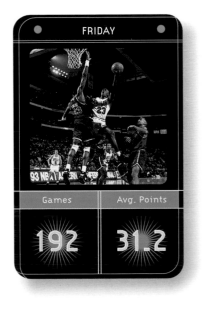

FRIDAY	
Games	Avg. Points
192	31.2

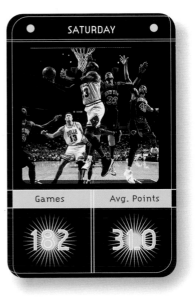

SATURDAY	
Games	Avg. Points
182	31.0

TOTALS	
Games	Avg. Points
930	31.5

THE CHICAGO BULLS WERE THE PERFECT TEAM FOR DENNIS RODMAN, AND PHIL JACKSON WAS THE PERFECT COACH.
PHIL ALLOWED DENNIS TO DO WHAT HE WANTED, BUT DENNIS KNEW HE HAD TO LOCK IN AND CONNECT

(E)ach of us had the freedom to be individuals and to exhibit our own unique personalities. Phil gave us that. He understood that putting restraints on players also took away some of the avenues players used to relax. Ultimately, that isn't good for the collective. Dennis was probably one of the reasons the wedge between Phil and management went so deep. Management gets nervous when players have the kind of freedom Dennis had. Krause never trusted players enough to provide that kind of space. Management was most comfortable with everyone on an even level with a single set of rules. Phil understood some players deserved more advantages than others. Dennis could go to Atlantic City and gamble all night and then plug in and get 25 rebounds. So he earned the freedom Phil granted him. Where did Phil come up with that philosophy? I have no idea. But I do know it was accepted and

respected by every player. If you showed him you could go your own way and still plug back into the team at game time, then he would allow you space. At the same time, if Phil ever felt those freedoms jeopardized our approach, he never had a problem pulling back the reins on anybody, including me, to bring the collective thought process back together. He was a player, he had been on championship teams, he had been in an environment with intelligent teammates who were independent and able to make choices. That's why Dennis found a home with the Bulls. That doesn't mean there weren't some harsh words from time to time. There were, usually from me. But our atmosphere allowed Dennis the freedom to be himself within the context of a professional basketball team trying to win championships. In that respect, the Chicago Bulls were unique.

IT SEEMED LIKE EVERYTHING HAD FALLEN INTO PLACE
FOR GAME 6 OF THE 1996 FINALS AGAINST SEATTLE.
I HAD COME BACK WITHOUT MY FATHER,
EVERYBODY WAS QUESTIONING WHAT I HAD DONE
UP TO THAT POINT AND WHAT MORE GRATIFICATION
COULD I POSSIBLY GET OTHER THAN

WINNING THE CHAMPIONSHIP ON FATHER'S DAY AS A

fourth

TRIBUTE TO MY FATHER.

(I)T COULDN'T HAVE PLAYED OUT ANY BETTER. I WAS SO DETERMINED THAT DAY. IT WAS LIKE SOMETIMES YOU GET SO ANGRY THAT YOU CRY. THAT'S HOW DETERMINED I WAS TO WIN THAT GAME. I WAS SO ANGRY AND SO HAPPY AT THE SAME TIME. THERE WAS NO WAY I COULD CONTROL MY EMOTIONS. I WAS ANGRY BECAUSE I FELT LIKE I HAD TO WIN ANOTHER CHAMPIONSHIP BEFORE ANYONE WOULD GIVE CREDENCE TO MY RETURN. BUT I WAS HAPPY THAT I PROVED MY POINT. I HAD LOVED THE GAME FOR SO LONG AND DONE SO MUCH IN THE GAME AND YET I WAS STILL BEING CRITICIZED. ONCE I GRABBED THAT BALL AND THE GAME WAS OVER IT HIT ME AS TO WHAT HAD JUST TRANSPIRED. I HAD COME ALL THE WAY BACK. THERE HAD BEEN SOME DISAPPOINTMENTS ALONG THE WAY, BUT THEY TAUGHT ME TO DO THE RIGHT THING. IF YOU DO THE WORK, YOU GET REWARDED. THERE ARE NO SHORTCUTS IN LIFE.

Jeff Malone was one of the toughest guys I played against during my career. I could play solid defense against him and he still could make big baskets. Mitch Richmond was definitely difficult for me. But Malone had a unique style. He had a great fallaway jump shot. Everything he did was a fallaway. I could play solid defense and he still could get that shot off. He was tough and he put up some solid numbers against me. Mitch plays well without the ball, he's savvy at the offensive end and he's strong. We had similar styles in that sense. From day one I liked Mitch. Just like from day one I liked Ray Allen because he has a lot of skills. Early in my career guys like World B Free and George Gervin gave me problems. I was young and I had never seen such smooth play. I had some good battles with Otis Birdsong and Micheal Ray Richardson. Alvin Robertson was tough. He always gambled on defense too much, though. He was real tough. He was a hands-on, scrappy-type player. Physically he'd bang you. Joe Dumars was tough but he always got help. He was very, very smart. Reggie Miller is tough because he knows how to get you into foul trouble and he's not afraid to take a shot from any distance. That's the thing about Reggie. Defensively, I didn't have a problem with Reggie. When I wanted to take advantage of Reggie physically I could do that offensively. He moves without the ball very well and he shoots quickly. He presented some problems, but once I got a feel for him I knew how to force him to his weakness.

THERE ARE ONLY A HANDFUL OF GUYS WHO UNDERSTAND HOW TO BE

PREDATORS

ON DEFENSE. SCOTTIE COMMITTED TO IT FROM DAY ONE.
THAT TOLD ME HE WAS SPECIAL.

VERY FEW GUYS COME INTO THE NBA WITH THE IDEA OF DOING ALL THE THANKLESS TASKS NECESSARY FOR A TEAM TO WIN. THEY USUALLY ARE FOCUSED ON SCORING POINTS AND PLAYING ENOUGH MINUTES TO PAD THEIR STATS.

(F)rom my perspective there are very, very few I came across in my career that I would consider to have achieved greatness. I would say Magic Johnson and Larry Bird achieved greatness to a certain extent. I learned from their example and took it a step further by becoming a factor at both ends of the court. The one player who I think is close to them is Scottie Pippen. He's an intelligent player, he understands the game. He had to learn how to be a warrior, how to be aggressive at all times, but Scottie did that. I've seen all facets of this game. It's not just what he can do offensively, but it's what Scottie Pippen can do defensively. He's right there with those guys except as a leader. Scottie has leadership qualities, but I didn't know if he wanted that role. In his defense, Scottie came from a smaller environment. It's like a kid growing up in the country playing against kids who grew up in the city. The kid in the country can learn, but it might take him a little longer. Bird and Magic came into the league ready to teach in some respects. Scottie came into the league ready to learn. Believe me, I don't think he's far from those guys. There were a lot of times on the court I felt like I was playing with my twin. That's how much he has grown in the time we played together. I still think I could break him down offensively and I have mastered some of the nuances of the game to a greater degree. But it's still a good match. He learned how to be a predator which meant attacking all the time, but still being able to surprise people. You never sit back and let yourself be attacked. The difference between us was Scottie was an attacker as long as he knew he had a pack of wolves with him. I'm an attacker without a pack of wolves. That's a big difference.

I COULD SEE THE FEAR IN THE EYES OF OTHER PLAYERS, ESPECIALLY WHEN THEY SAID SOMETHING THEY WEREN'T SURE THEY COULD BACK UP.

Let's say someone swears he's going to play better the next night. But once the game starts that player misses his first shot. At that moment you can detect the slightest hesitation, the first hint of fear. Instead of looking at the situation and saying, "OK, I have a good feel for the game now. I'll make the next one," one negative starts building upon another. It's like they start building this wall, one negative piled upon another, until they have no chance of finding a way to knock it down. If I missed a shot, so what? I had the freedom to accept the consequence. I wasn't going to let a missed shot or a mistake affect the rest of my night. I never allowed the negatives to carry over and pile up. In those moments I relied upon past experience. I'd go back to games where I missed my first five shots and then made the next ten. I would try to bring that confidence into the moment. By staying in the moment I was never focused on what might happen two or three minutes later, which meant I wasn't thinking about the negative possibility of missing another shot. Why would I worry about a shot I hadn't even taken yet? That kind of thinking limits everyone, not just athletes. They aren't comfortable with their skills and they don't have a good connection with their inner being. I tried to improve each and every day. I needed to be able to look back to yesterday and feel like I'm better today. During the game it was a matter of keeping your poise, learning how to settle your nerves in the heat of the moment. I would look for easy opportunities to set the tone, to settle my mind, so I could let the game come to me instead of chasing it all night. That's one of the differences between a good player and a great one.

WHEN I WAS A KID I ALWAYS LIKED TO DRESS UP ON SUNDAYS.
MY BROTHERS AND SISTERS WANTED TO WEAR JEANS, BUT I WORE A COAT AND TIE. FROM MY PERSPECTIVE, I VIEWED WEARING A COAT AND TIE AS BEING DRESSED UP.

I REMEMBER MY FATHER TELLING ME HOW
IMPORTANT FIRST IMPRESSIONS CAN BE FOR SOME PEOPLE.
AT NORTH CAROLINA WE WORE SUITS EVERY TIME
WE TRAVELED, AND THAT WAS RIGHT UP MY ALLEY.
WE WERE TRAVELING TOGETHER AND WE WANTED TO LOOK
PRESENTABLE, DIGNIFIED. THAT'S WHY I TOOK THE TIME
TO GET COMPLETELY DRESSED IN MY ROOM BEFORE
LEAVING FOR THE ARENA. I WANTED TO PRESENT MYSELF
IN A WAY THAT WOULD GIVE PEOPLE THE PROPER
IMPRESSION OF ME. I WANTED THEM TO KNOW
I CARED ABOUT WHAT THEY THOUGHT. IN A SMALL WAY,
I WAS ABLE TO SHOW MY RESPECT FOR THEM, TOO.

THE ONE THING I WOULD TELL YOUNGER PLAYERS IS TO ENJOY THE MOMENT AND BE CAREFUL NOT TO PUT THEMSELVES INTO A BOX OTHERS HAVE ERECTED FOR THEM. SUCCESS WILL BREED HIGHER EXPECTATIONS, BUT THAT'S JUST A NATURAL EVOLUTION IN OUR SOCIETY. YOU HAVE TO KNOW WHO YOU ARE BEFORE YOU CAN GROW AS A PERSON AND A PLAYER.

LOOK AT KOBE BRYANT. HE DOESN'T EVEN KNOW WHAT KOBE BRYANT'S GAME IS YET. HOW COULD HE?

HE WENT FROM HIGH SCHOOL TO AN ENVIRONMENT IN WHICH HE HAS TO SINK OR SWIM. HE'S BEEN ABLE TO GET BY ON RAW PHYSICAL ABILITY, BUT HE NEEDS TO DEVELOP HIS OWN FOUNDATION BEFORE HE CAN BECOME A GREAT PLAYER. HE CAN GET BY BORROWING FROM OTHER PLAYERS IN THE SHORT TERM, BUT SOONER OR LATER HE WILL HAVE TO FIND HIS OWN GAME. THAT'S WHY COLLEGE IS SO IMPORTANT. IF I HAD COME RIGHT OUT OF HIGH SCHOOL INTO THE NBA I DON'T THINK I WOULD HAVE BECOME THE SAME PLAYER. I WOULDN'T HAVE HAD THAT FOUNDATION THAT NORTH CAROLINA PROVIDED. AT THE PROFESSIONAL LEVEL YOU HAVE TO PRODUCE. I WOULD HAVE FOUND WAYS TO COMPETE NIGHT AFTER NIGHT INSTEAD OF DEVELOPING A LONG-TERM PLAN.

CAN KOBE BRYANT BECOME A

SURE. BUT IT'S GOING TAKE A LOT MORE EFFORT TO REFINE HIS SKILLS AT THE SAME TIME HE'S TRYING TO SURVIVE.

GREAT PLAYER?

Young players also need to know what makes them happy off the floor. What brightens your day? I don't think a lot of players ever gain that knowledge about themselves. They think they know. They think watching videos, going out to clubs, or hanging out with a different woman every night is the answer. If that's what you think makes you truly happy, then you're going to get burned, because it's fleeting. What are you left with when that's been your focus night after night? Those are the kinds of things I try to tell young players. Those are the kinds of conversations I have with Tiger Woods, too. Slow down. Enjoy life. Take it easy. Don't make it difficult. I think with all that was thrown at Tiger so quickly, he felt, quite naturally, that he had to live up to the hype. No one can live up

to that kind of hype. I learned that a long time ago. It's something Tiger will have to learn if he wants to perform at a high level and maintain that level for a long time. When I was 21 I was still eating McDonald's food every day. I wasn't trying to search for the perfect meal, for the perfect attitude, or the perfect technique. It just happened. That was the beauty of it all. These guys need to learn to live for the moment. Let it flow and see what happens. There is only so much you can control anyway. If you don't enjoy the process of becoming successful, then there is no beauty in the achievement. Enjoy the day. There will be another one tomorrow. Enjoy life for the sake of life

IF I KNEW THEN WHAT I KNOW NOW

about what I would have to go through in Game 5 of the 1997 Finals at Utah,

I DON'T KNOW IF I WOULD PLAY.

If the outcome was guaranteed to be the same, then I'd probably go through it again.

But if the outcome wasn't assured, there's no way I would do it again.

fifth

I COULD HAVE DIED FOR A BASKETBALL GAME.

I PLAYED THAT GAME ON HEART AND DETERMINATION AND NOTHING ELSE.

I didn't have any food, any energy, any sleep, or anything else. I don't even remember a lot about that game.

I have never felt as awful physically as I did in that game.

Ⓘ woke up at three in the morning with what seemed like stomach flu. I couldn't keep anything down and I couldn't sleep. I took something that I thought would make me drowsy, but the symptoms were so severe I never got back to sleep. By the time I got to the arena I was fighting to stay awake.

I just sat back in the locker room drinking coffee, trying to wake up enough to play the game. I didn't have anything in my stomach and the coffee really didn't do anything to wake me up. By halftime I was getting dehydrated, so I started drinking what I thought was Gatorade. But someone had mistakenly handed me a bottle of GatorLode, which  is what you are supposed to drink after you have finished a difficult activity. By the time we went back out for the second half I felt bloated on top of being exhausted. I had con- tinued to drink coffee, which ultimately only helped the dehydration come more quickly. There were times in the third and fourth quarters that I felt like I was going to pass out. I remember thinking, "Get this game over so I can lie down." In the fourth quarter, right before the three-pointer that won the game, I had become almost completely dehydrated. I was shivering, but I continued to sweat. On that last shot, I didn't even know whether it went in or not. I could barely stand up. When I got back into the locker room the doctors were really concerned because I didn't have anything left. I was cold, yet I was sweating and dehydrated. They wanted to give me intravenous fluids, but I made it over to a table, lay down, and started drinking Gatorade. That's all I did for about 45 minutes. All for a basketball game.

The Bulls knew I wouldn't come back and play for anyone but Phil. After the 1997 championship, they knew they had to sign Phil before they went after me. But they put a clause in Phil's contract that said if I didn't sign by a certain date Phil's deal was void. When we started negotiating my contract for the 1997–98 season everyone knew what I had made the year before. David Falk told the Bulls I deserved a 20 percent raise, the maximum allowed. His feeling was that I had done everything I was paid to do. We won another cham-

pionship, I won another scoring title, I made the All-Defensive First Team. Jerry's opinion was that I had been paid a lot of money for that performance and I shouldn't get anything more. The discussion eventually went all the way back to my first two contracts and how I wasn't paid market value at the time, so these kinds of numbers were in order to balance the sheets. Finally, I said, "Look, Jerry. My agent is here. You are here. Why don't we split it down the middle, shake hands and get out of here. I'm not out here trying to rob you. I want you to know I lived up to my end of the bargain. I did

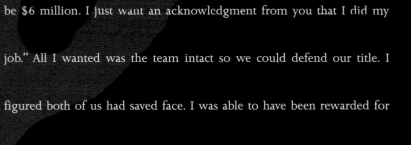

my job and all I'm asking for is a raise. That could be a dollar or that could be $6 million. I just want an acknowledgment from you that I did my job." All I wanted was the team intact so we could defend our title. I figured both of us had saved face. I was able to have been rewarded for my performance and Jerry was able to say, "OK, we paid you a lot of money, but we also have rewarded you with a number we feel comfortable with." My first thought was, "Great. Now let's go out and do it again." But I knew it never should have come to that kind of discussion. We should have been way past that point, particularly after what happened the year before. Following the 1996 season I signed a one-year deal. Before I left the room, Jerry said something I'll never forget. It changed my opinion of Jerry Reinsdorf. We shook hands and he said, "At some point in time, I know I'm going to regret what we just did." After all these years, after all these championships, after all I had tried to do for the Bulls organization, after all those years of being underpaid and you regret paying me market value? It was like a punch in the heart.

I KEPT **SIX** PAIRS OF EVERY AIR JORDAN SHOE.

MADISON SQUARE GARDEN	FIRST AND LAST GAME BOX SCORE								
FIRST GAME—November 8, 1984: Bulls 121-Knicks 106									

Chicago Bulls starting lineup: Steve Johnson(F), Orlando Woolridge(F), Caldwell Jones(C), Ennis Whatley(G).

M	FGM	FGA	FTM	FTA	RB	AST	STL	BLK	PTS
33	15	22	3	4	8	5	3	2	33

LAST GAME—March 8, 1998: Bulls 102-Knicks 89									

Chicago Bulls starting lineup: Scottie Pippen(F), Toni Kukoc(F), Dennis Rodman(C), Ron Harper(G).

M	FGM	FGA	FTM	FTA	RB	AST	STL	BLK	PTS
43	17	33	7	9	8	6	3	1	42

THE NIGHT BEFORE WE WERE LEAVING TO PLAY OUR LAST GAME IN NEW YORK IN 1998, MY WIFE WAS DOING SOME SPRING CLEANING AND MOVED THE SHOES FROM ONE STORAGE CLOSET TO ANOTHER. I THOUGHT,

"THIS MIGHT BE MY LAST TIME IN NEW YORK. LET'S GO BACK TO THE BEGINNING AND WEAR THESE SHOES."

I had worn them before in practice and I thought they were too tight. But it was New York—why not try something different? No one knew I had the shoes in my bag until I started lacing them up. I didn't know for sure I'd wear them in the game until after I tried them out in warm-ups. By then the shoes had caught people's attention, so why not go with it? That's how I approached the game. I wanted to go out there and have a good time. It was a heck of a statement about my feelings for New York. I appreciated playing in New York from the beginning to the end. Plus, we won the game. Their tribute to me was the standing ovation they gave me when I left the court.

sixth

(E)verything leading up to the shot against Utah in Game 6 of the 1998 Finals was vivid. It was like I was watching everything unfold in slow motion on television. I stole the ball, looked up at the clock, and then down the court. I could see every player and I remember exactly where they were as I came up the floor. Steve Kerr was in the corner, John Stockton faked at me and was going to come to me. I was up top. Dennis was curling underneath the post on the left. Scottie was on the bottom post on the right. I could hear sounds, but it was like white noise. In that moment I couldn't distinguish one sound from another, but I was able to evaluate every opportunity on the court. I was going to the right because I knew I could get a shot off. Any time I needed to make a shot I went to my right as long as the defense didn't make a mistake and open a lane to my left. When you go to your right the defensive player has to come across your body to get to the ball.

In Game 1 of the 1997 NBA Finals against Utah, I went left when I hit the game-winning shot because Byron Russell lunged to his left, causing him to be off balance. In 1998, I set myself up to go right again, starting on the left side of the floor. The one thing I didn't want to do was cross over because that would put the ball back into play. All this I knew, but as the shot unfolded, I went through those options instinctively. It unfolded slowly enough for me to evaluate every single thing that was happening. I was able

to evaluate the mistake Russell made again and capitalize differently. When he lunged this time I knew exactly what to do. I was going toward Steve Kerr. John Stockton wasn't about to leave Steve open as he had when Steve hit the winning shot in Game 6 of the 1997 Finals. So Stockton faked toward me and went back to Kerr. I had no intention of passing the ball under any circumstances. I figured I stole the ball and it was my opportunity to win or lose the game. I would have taken that shot with five people on me. Ironically, I have problems going to my right for a stop, pull-up jumper because I have a tendency to come up short. I normally fade a little. But on this shot I didn't want to fade because all my jump shots had been short. Think about that. I had enough time to think about those issues. It's incredible, even to me. And yet, that's how it happened. I went straight up and I came straight down.

I consciously extended my hand up and out toward the target because I had been coming up short. It looked like I was posing, but it was a fundamentally sound shot. It's truly amazing that I can break down a game into all those parts in that amount of time and then execute the play.

ALL THAT HAPPENED IN ABOUT 11 SECONDS.

WHEN THE NEWS BROKE
DURING THE SUMMER ABOUT
THE BULLS HIRING TIM FLOYD
I WAS DOING MY
BASKETBALL CAMP AT
ELMHURST COLLEGE OUTSIDE
CHICAGO. WE WOULD HAVE
A QUESTION-AND-ANSWER
PERIOD WITH THE KIDS.
USUALLY THEY WOULD ASK
WHAT KIND OF GUM I CHEWED,
STUFF LIKE THAT.
**ONE OF THEM ASKED ME WHY
I DIDN'T WANT TO PLAY
FOR A COACH OTHER THAN
PHIL JACKSON.**
I SAID, "LET ME GIVE YOU
A COMPARISON. IF YOU GREW
UP YOUR ENTIRE LIFE
WITH ONE SET OF PARENTS AND
YOU GOT TO A CERTAIN AGE AND
YOU WERE ASSIGNED NEW PARENTS,
WHAT WOULD YOU WANT?
WOULD YOU WANT TO STAY WITH
YOUR ORIGINAL PARENTS OR
WITH THE NEW PARENTS?
THE OLD PARENTS WERE THE PEOPLE
WHO TAUGHT YOU EVERYTHING,
FED YOU, HELPED YOU THROUGH
CERTAIN PERIODS OF YOUR LIFE.
NOW THEY SAY YOU HAVE TO GO
THROUGH THE SAME PROCESS
WITH NEW PARENTS?"
THAT'S HOW I FEEL ABOUT PLAYING
FOR ANOTHER COACH.

ALTHOUGH IT WOULD HAVE BEEN HARD TO PLAY FOR ANOTHER COACH,
I ALWAYS WONDERED HOW IT WOULD HAVE BEEN TO PLAY FOR NEW YORK.
GIVEN THE FACTS OF PHIL'S DEPARTURE AND THE BULLS' DESIRE TO REBUILD, I WOULD HAVE SERIOUSLY CONSIDERED PLAYING FOR THE KNICKS DURING THE 1998-99 SEASON IF I WERE SINGLE.
NEW YORK FANS APPRECIATE GOOD PLAYERS AND I ALWAYS ENJOYED PLAYING IN MADISON SQUARE GARDEN.

TOMORROW I DON'T KNOW WHAT I'M GOING TO DO. I THINK ABOUT TODAY. PEOPLE DON'T BELIEVE I DON'T KNOW WHAT'S GOING TO HAPPEN NEXT WEEK, NEXT MONTH, OR NEXT YEAR.

BUT I TRULY LIVE IN THE MOMENT.

That's what retirement means. You can design and choose your moment. I can design shoes one day and ski the next. I have created the opportunity to have a choice. That is how I am going to live. I am not going to determine what the moment is going to be a week from now. I've never done that and I don't like living that way. I would feel too confined. To me, retirement is having no restraints. I won't be retired fully until I don't have to do anything. One day I won't have to do commercials, or talk to a board, or help in the design of shoes. I will be able to wake up when I wake up. As long as I live in the moment I don't believe I will ever get bored. I am not going to mind being out of the spotlight.

MY PROBLEM IS THAT EVERYONE EXPECTS ME TO LIVE IN THE FUTURE.

Where did it come from? I don't know. That's like asking an artist where his inspiration comes from. Phil Jackson told us many times to deal with what's happening right now. It's an idea that always has been with me. My heart and my soul are in the moment. The best thing about living that way is that you don't know what the next moment is going to bring. And that was the best thing about the way I played the game. No one, not even me, knew what I was going to do next. If I had to pick one characteristic about my game that would be it. I always thought I performed my best when I didn't know what was coming. I didn't know I was going to go out there and score 63 points against the Boston Celtics in my second season. They didn't either and that's why it was a beautiful experience. No one could have expected that to happen. They were stunned, just like I was. What's more beautiful than that?

I CAN'T SAY THERE ISN'T AN EGO BOOST OR A HIGHER SENSE OF CONFIDENCE IN YOURSELF WHEN YOU HAVE HAD AS MANY LIGHTS SHINING ON YOU AS I HAVE HAD. **BUT I NEVER BELIEVED ALL THE PRESS CLIPPINGS AND I NEVER FOUND COMFORT IN THE SPOTLIGHT.** I DON'T KNOW HOW YOU CAN AND NOT LOSE YOUR WORK ETHIC.